Praise for *A Story Worth Telling*

"Now here's a book that will help you n
Blankschaen doesn't just challenge you to
paints a picture of what a life fully alive looks like. Don't miss this."
— *Jeff Goins, author,* The Art of Work

"People who live a story worth telling start with authentic faith. Want your life to resonate? Want to become a catalyst for lasting change? Wish you had the courage to pursue your true calling and God-given dreams? Read this book!" — *Brad Lomenick, author of* The Catalyst Leader *and* H3 Leadership, *former President of Catalyst*

"A life of significance is a life propelled by authentic faith. This book will show you how to make your life story the best God intended for it to be." — *Mark Sanborn, President of Sanborn & Associates, Inc. and author of* The Fred Factor *and* Fred 2.0

"The Gospel is good news, and Bill Blankschaen's book describes just how good it is. Read this book to be equipped and inspired to see your life differently. And I suspect you'll want to share it with others." — *John Stonestreet, speaker and fellow, The Chuck Colson Center for Christian Worldview; Senior Content Advisor, Summit Ministries*

"In *A Story Worth Telling*, Bill Blankschaen challenges and inspires us to write our story deliberately, authentically, and faithfully. Read and act on the ideas Bill shares and chapters of your own life will soon be inspiring others to live a life of lasting significance." — *Skip Prichard, Blogger at Leadership Insights (SkipPrichard.com)*

"We live in a time when fervent faith in biblical truth is increasingly under attack. More than ever, what you believe matters. In *A Story Worth Telling*, Bill inspires us to use truth the way God intended—liberated from theological textbooks on apologetics and applied to the practical world of everyday life. Read this book to take your faith to where it could and should be!" — *Kelly Monroe Kullberg, author of* Finding God at Harvard; *Founder, The Veritas Forum; Developer, The America Conservancy*

"Wow! What an encouraging read! One of my primary goals as a pastor is to encourage people to 'get out of the boat and walk on water'— whenever and wherever God calls. *A Story Worth Telling* challenges us to live a life of authentic faith and follow after God with everything in us. Easy to read and packed full of inspiration, you'll definitely want to read it again." —*Ron Edmondson, Pastor, Blogger (RonEdmondson .com), Church Leadership Consultant*

"Safety and security are overrated; we were created to live for far more than merely our own comfort. In *A Story Worth Telling*, Bill explores biblical truths that will challenge and equip any reader to break free from monotony and live a better story. Don't wait! Read this book and begin a new chapter of your life's adventure." —*Peter Greer, President & CEO, HOPE International; coauthor of* Mission Drift

"Do you often find your life to be a persistent plod on the treadmill of monotony while feeling in your gut you were created for so much more? Jesus has promised life to the full, but you'll only find the abundant life when you faithfully yield your story to the grand redemptive story of God. Lace up your boots and let Bill guide you on an exhilarating journey of faith. The abundant life you're seeking is just up around the bend—if only you're willing to get off the treadmill and onto the trail!" —*Jason Haynes, Director of Content, Catalyst*

"When I first saw the title of this book, *A Story Worth Telling*, I wondered if this would be one more Christian book telling me all the things I need to do to make my life more interesting. Yes, this book is wonderfully practical, with tangible actions I can take. But the focus is not on me and what I must do, but on God and what it means for me to have a vital, growing, active faith in God. Through his engaging, biblically based wisdom, Bill Blankschaen will refresh your faith in God through Jesus Christ, guiding you into living a compelling story, not because of your efforts, but because of God's grace experienced through faith." —*Mark D. Roberts, Executive Director of the Max De Pree Center for Leaders, Fuller Theological Seminary*

"Few Christian writers combine theological acumen, devotional fervor, vocational insight, cultural savvy, and absorbing narrative as Bill Blankschaen does. This work is a veritable handbook on success in the Christian life—not superficial success of popular self-improvement manuals clothed in a thin Christian veneer, but godly success anchored in the truths of the joyous Christian revelation. In our culture imbued with a bleak outlook for far too many Christians, Bill proposes a destination of hope and joy and expectation in Jesus Christ—and shows us how to get there." —*P. Andrew Sandlin, President, The Center for Cultural Leadership*

"Bill Blankschaen has a gift. Combining deep insight with vivid, memorable, and practical illustrations, he shows that biblical faith is not just the entrance gate to the kingdom of heaven; it is also the vehicle, the engine, and the road. Faith isn't just the way to life, it is the way of life. This book is a delightful guide to getting the most out of your faith and your life." —*Brian Mattson, Senior Scholar of Public Theology, Center For Cultural Leadership; Producer and Principal, Dead Reckoning Digital Network (www.deadreckoning.tv)*

"In *A Story Worth Telling*, Bill provides a helpful guide to living the kind of faithful, authentic life we all desire. No matter what stage of your life you are in, this book will help you live with meaning in the here and now. I recommend this book to everyone who wants to make the most of the time they've been given." —*Michael Wear, Consultant, Speaker, Writer, and Former White House Staffer*

"When it comes to walking by faith, risk aversion is not a badge of honor. *A Story Worth Telling* is just the challenge my Millenial generation needs to step out in bold and confident faith. Deep down, this is the story that all of us want to live. Bill asks the hard questions that can catapult us into a riskier, more God-honoring faith walk that will echo through all eternity." —*Amanda Sanchez, Executive Director of CaCHE Global, Entrepreneur*

"After the first few chapters of *A Story Worth Telling*, I thought of William Wallace's quote in *Braveheart*, 'Every man dies. Not every man truly lives.' This book is an instruction manual for truly living a life of meaning and purpose. I was challenged and inspired by it, and you will be too—if you steep in its wisdom and do what you've never done before." —*Tor Constantino, former journalist, best-selling author and contributor to Entrepreneur and The Good Men Project*

"Bill Blankschaen writes with the voice of that friend we all want to have: the wise and engaging, pleasant and humorous friend you could talk to all night just for the fun of it. *A Story Worth Telling* challenges us to live always in the light of our eternal destiny. Bill calls us to live an extraordinary story, not to curry the favor of the world, but so that our life here will be consistent with our life there: one consistent story of pursuing and glorifying God. It's a great shift of perspective, and I hope many people read the book and enjoy it as much as I did."
—*Timothy Dalrymple, Author and Entrepreneur*

"Faith is what led Abram to leave his home. It's what led Moses to raise his staff. But the lack of faith is what led Israel into exile. In *A Story Worth Telling*, Bill Blankschaen outlines the need for continuing faith, for salvation and beyond. Answer Bill's call for taking steps

toward abundant faith and, Scripture assures you, God will meet you there. Pick up this book not only to receive a faith challenge, but also to help you see what faith looks like in the practical areas of life."
—*Tyler Braun, pastor, New Harvest Church, Salem, Oregon; author of* Why Holiness Matters

"At the crossroads of daring to set out into the unknown or slumping back into your comfortable life, you will find *A Story Worth Telling*, Bill Blankschaen's thrilling contemplation on faith. He writes convincingly about the modern Christian's dilemma: How do I step out in faith in the midst of a comfortable culture of convenience? I commend this book to you as one that will challenge you to gain a 'holy discomfort' as you live out active faith." —*Steve Smothermon, Senior Pastor, Legacy Church, Albuquerque, NM; author of* Big Problems, Bigger God.

"Reading a good story inspires greater stories to be told. Bill does more than just tell his story; he guides you to write your own. Living a story may not seem safe, but faith isn't about safe. It's about resting on the character of God who Himself provides infinite security. Let Bill lovingly push you out of the boat because he knows from experience that God can and must be trusted completely if He is to be trusted at all." —*Mark Spansel, Lead Pastor, Leroy Community Chapel*

"If salvation is actually a process and heaven really isn't downhill, then we should all listen and let Bill Blankschaen guide us to live a life that matters, to live what we say we believe." —*Dan Nichols, Lead Pastor, Restored Church*

"God has chapters written for our lives filled with adventure, hope, and promise. But do we have the courage to turn the page? Bill cuts to the heart of what it means to follow Jesus. *A Story Worth Telling* will help move your faith from your head to your heart—and to your feet." —*Jason Tucker, Senior Pastor, Tower Hill Church*

"It is possible to recapture your intimate and active walk of faith with Jesus! With piercing effectiveness, *A Story Worth Telling* equips us to lay hold of the audacious journey God intends for all Christ-followers. Bill helps us courageously dip our toe in the water and experience the power of God." —*Daniel Buell, President, Cornerstone Christian Academy*

"Talk about a wake-up call! If you're tired of living a life of pretending, *A Story Worth Telling* dares you to live a life filled with adventurous faith. Let Bill guide you to attempt the improbable so you can do the impossible." —*Kenny Jahng, Church Online Pastor, Liquid Church*

A STORY
WORTH
TELLING

FAITH ▶ WALKERS

Your Field Guide to Living an Authentic Life

BILL BLANKSCHAEN

ABINGDON PRESS
NASHVILLE

*To my wife, Faith, and our children—for believing,
and to my mother and father for living a story of
faithful service to Christ.*

A Story Worth Telling
Your Field Guide to Living an Authentic Life

Copyright © 2015 by William B. Blankschaen

Library of Congress Cataloging-in-Publication Data

Blankschaen, Bill.
    Live a story worth telling : a faithwalker's guide / Bill Blankschaen.
       pages cm
    Includes bibliographical references and index.
    ISBN 978-1-4267-8643-3 (binding: soft back : alk. paper)   1. Christian life.   I. Title.
    BV4501.3.B5425 2015
    248.4—dc23

                                                          2015004790

15 16 17 18 19 20 21 22 23 24—10 9 8 7 6 5 4 3 2 1

MANUFACTURED IN THE UNITED STATES OF AMERICA

CONTENTS

YOU CAN CHOOSE YOUR STORY

S tories: there's no escaping them, and who would want to? The world runs on tales of conflict and romance! Television thrives on them. Marketers squeeze them into thirty-second spots. Politicians manufacture them. Journalists seek an "angle" while sports broadcasters claim to have the "inside story" behind competing teams. We watch other people live stories through reality TV and idolize celebrities who appear to have stories of glamour and success. We share briefly in their joy or pain—even when their stories end tragically, or they get voted off the island—then turn to the next prepackaged talent, hoping to discover another escapade we can pretend to live, if only for fleeting moments.

And that's the key, isn't it? We love stories because we long to experience one of our own, to take an expedition that requires the courage to dream for a cause we believe in, even in the face of great risk. We want our lives to become dramatic tales of adventure and danger in which we face imminent peril, take on impossible challenges—instead of pretending that our story actually means something.

But what if you didn't have to pretend? What if you didn't have to borrow someone else's adventure? What if you could live a story worth telling, a life of such lasting significance that the account of your life would not just be told but celebrated in places and times you cannot now imagine? Is that a journey you'd be interested in taking? Wait—before you answer, there's something you should know: talking about living a story worth telling and actually doing it are very different things. Talking requires little; living demands more. Living a story worth telling requires you to step into the unknown, a place where you have no idea what will happen next. It calls you to confront your deepest fears, biggest personal giants, and darkest villains. The journey demands that you endure the discomfort of change and the potential for deep disappointment. In short, living a story worth telling is not easy. That's why most people settle for a story that is anything but worth telling. They choose safety over significance, comfort over lasting legacy. But as John C. Maxwell says, "Security does not give purpose." Gail Sheehy, author of *Passages,* captures the choice each of us must make:

> If we don't change, we don't grow. If we don't grow, we are not really living. Growth demands a temporary surrender of security. It may mean a giving up of familiar but limiting patterns, safe but unrewarding work, values no longer believed in, relationships that have lost their meaning. As Dostoevsky put it, "taking a new step, uttering a new word, is what

people fear most." The real fear should be the opposite course.

It's true that stories can be unpredictable—that is often why
we like them. But they are also inescapable. If you're breathing,
you're living a story now. The plot unfolds with each breath you
take. The question is not will you live a story, but will your story
be worth telling?

A SOAP-BUBBLE LIFE

Here in the second decade of the twenty-first century, thinking our stories could be worth telling might strike some people
as odd. We've grown up getting trophies for merely showing up,
so to suggest that some stories have more value than others may
seem elitist. We live in a day when those who celebrate success
too loudly are decried as being inconsiderate of the less fortu-
nate. And those who suggest one value or perspective is supe-
rior to another are derided as intolerant. Consequently, we de-
mean the value of everything—even of value itself—by insisting
that all outcomes be valued equally. As Steven Garber recently
phrased it, many of us embrace the cultural slogan of *whatever*.
We're not happy with where that perspective leaves us, nor does
it actually work in reality, but *whatever*. Even though we sense
a deeper purpose that calls us to live a greater story, we resign
ourselves to living a meaningless tale, going with the flow as a
river's currents conform to rocky banks.

American cultural commentator Mark Twain accurately described this cynical view of life more than a century ago:

3

We are blown upon the world; we float buoyantly upon the summer air a little while, complacently showing off our grace of form and our dainty iridescent colors; then we vanish with a little puff, leaving nothing behind but a memory—and sometimes not even that. I suppose that at those solemn times when we wake in the deeps of the night and reflect, there is not one of us who is not willing to confess that he is really only a soap-bubble, and as little worth the making.

Truth be told, our worst fear is that we will live and die and our lives will have made no difference to anyone. We're afraid that we will be just soap bubbles that floated for a bit, then— pop! Nothing but splotches evaporating in the inevitable heat of the next inevitable day. Is this cultural pressure to run from meaning really the story you want? Living a story worth telling will produce the greatest joy possible, even as it tests your courage. Your life can mean more than you can imagine, because no one dreams of a soap-bubble life. But what do you dream of? Take a moment now to pause and reconnect with those dreams.

 ## CHECK YOUR COORDINATES

Are you living a story worth telling? Before we move forward, check your coordinates to see where you are on the journey:

- Where do you feel tension now between your dreams and the appearance of safety and security?

- What does living a soap-bubble life, a life of indifference, look like to you?

- Where might your life be showing signs of suds?

THE CHOICE IS ALL YOURS

Here's the great news: you can *choose* to live a story worth telling! No matter where you find yourself in life right now, you can reach the place where you know your story matters. Today you may be energized by apparent success, discouraged by soul-wrenching failure, uncertain about your next move, or crippled by suffering that has left you with little hope. On the other hand, you may be completely comfortable with your life, wondering why your friend gave you this book and why you would ever choose a more challenging existence. But no matter your starting point, you can take the journey to live a story worth telling, my friend. You can begin now. And you don't need to do it alone.

This book is intended to serve as your field guide for stepping out of your comfort zone and into the adventure of a story worth telling. So lace up your hiking boots and prepare to pack for the journey—it's not for the faint of heart, but nothing worthwhile ever is. And just because you *can* live a more meaningful life doesn't mean you *will*. You must consciously *choose* it. Existing is all about drifting downstream, going with the flow, rolling down the path of least resistance. Living a dynamic, fulfilling story promises something grander: the opportunity to connect with something bigger than we can even imagine. It requires leaving the well-worn paths and off-roading through life in ways that often make little sense to those simply existing around us.

Adventure means groping through the thickest mists, braving the deepest valleys, and scaling the steepest cliffs in order to achieve what most say is impossible. Sure, it will be difficult. But let's face it: the worst stories aren't the ones with sad endings or tragic denouements. No, the worst stories are those that seem to lack any point at all. They drift in random directions like soap bubbles, leaving us confused at best, bored at worst, but mostly just frustrated that we wasted time listening.

When we think about the stories we love to tell and retell, they are not tales of drifting, but of intentional living in pursuit of a higher purpose. They're not tales of comfort and ease, but of tension and risk. The heroes we cheer are the characters who believe in something of value, something worth fighting for. They act on what they believe to be true, often in spite of discomfort, fear, and uncertainty—and that makes their stories worth telling.

Perhaps most important, the heroes are normal, everyday people like you and me who at one point thought it impossible to live a story worth telling. They had to opt between settling for the way things were or carving out a new path to the way things should be. They hoped, like Frodo Baggins in *The Lord of the Rings*, that someone else would take the Ring so they could return to their peaceful Shire. Like the demure princess Esther, they dreaded asking for a favor that could save lives but cost everything. Like the disabled soldier in *Avatar*, they thought themselves unfit to take on a greedy military industrial machine to save a peaceful, native people. But they all chose to act on what they believed to be true and become heroes of stories we love to celebrate.

So what's the secret? What's the difference between conventional folk and heroes? It's simple: ordinary people learn to live stories worth telling *by walking with extraordinary faith*. And so can you.

 ## Prepare Your Gear

You can choose your story, but it requires intentional living. Here are five questions to help you identify if your life has begun to drift:

1. **What are you most looking forward to in life?** All too many people live for the weekend, the next vacation, or a break of some sort. Wouldn't it be better to live a story that doesn't make you want to run away?

2. **Are you self-medicating?** When we're not happy with our life direction, but are afraid to do anything about it, we tend to mask the frustration with stuff that gives a sense of temporary fulfillment or escape.

3. **What is your purpose?** If you haven't yet invested time in developing a personal mission statement, now would be good time to get the clarity you need.

4. **How often do you use the words *I can't*?** When you find your default answer is that four-letter word *can't*, you may have fallen into the drifting habit.

5. **Could someone identify your dreams by examining your life?** Steven Pressfield says many of us settle for a "shadow calling," something that looks enough like our true calling to make us feel better about not following our dreams.

FAITH IS...

One of my favorite places on earth to be is Walt Disney World in Orlando, Florida. The story behind the happiest place on earth and one man who saw what others failed to see is one we'll visit in future chapters. But for now, I want to focus on this: as much as I love spending time with my family at the Magic Kingdom, one message I often hear there simply rings hollow. It's when Jiminy Cricket says, "If only you believe!" at the end of every night. "Wishes can come true if you believe in them with all your heart. And the best part is you'll never run out of wishes. 'When you wish upon a star...make a wish and your dreams will come true.'" As much as I enjoy the fireworks that close the show at Disney World (they're second to none), I can't help but ask myself: Do all these people actually think that if they just believe, they can have anything they desire? Do you believe that? Should I?

Many people, sometimes even you and I, think that's what faith must be: a crazy leap into the unknown while you hope that fate, or at least Pinocchio's Blue Fairy, will step in and see you through. But life is too short for that. You might as well trust that Santa will give you the first gift of Christmas at the

North Pole if only you choose to get on a train. Such notions are not about faith, but fairy tales.

While some mistake faith for fairy tales, others mistake faith for religion. Religion is intended to support and strengthen faith, though it can also hinder and derail over time. All of us know religious people living stories that are as dull and forgettable as they come. Being religious doesn't mean that you are living with authentic faith—or living a story worth telling.

What's the difference? J. M. Barrie, author of the book *Peter Pan* on which the Disney tale was based, came a little closer to reality: "All the world is made of faith, and trust, and pixie dust." Except for the pixie dust, he got pretty close to capturing just how essential faith is to everything. The need to trust is woven into the very fabric of the universe. And that is why faith, rightly focused, is essential to living a story worth telling.

If faith is not fairy-tale belief and it isn't religion, then what is it? I offer this definition:

Faith is doing what you believe to be true, often in spite of what you see, sense, or feel. Sorry, no feel-good maxims or pixie dust. But no complicated theological-textbook words either. When it comes down to it, faith isn't all that complicated. We'll unpack this simple definition in the pages to come, but for now, note the three main ingredients:

1. **Doing.** Our stories will be determined by what we do. That seems obvious enough. A little less obvious is that what we *do* is determined by what we *believe* to be true. Until we act on what we say we believe, we don't really know what we believe. In those times

when our actions bring challenging consequences, we discover what our faith actually is. Our motion reveals our devotion to what we believe to be true.

2. **What you believe to be true.** Think back on the stories you love. Aren't they stories of heroes who took on the impossible because of something they believed in, whether cause, person, country, or dream? Think of Captain America's renegade band that preserves freedom for all and saves the world from doom in *The Winter Soldier*. Or of Marcus Luttrell's true story of loyalty to country and comrades in the mountains of Afghanistan, as vividly portrayed in the film *Lone Survivor*. Few stories resonate with us like those whose characters laid it all on the line for what they believed. Visionaries like Walt Disney, humanitarians like Mother Teresa, and even ambitious entrepreneurs such as Steve Jobs were motivated by what they believed to be true about life and their own unique roles in it.

3. **Often in spite of what you see, sense, or feel.** Living with abundant faith does not mean that what you believe must always contradict what you see. Too often we make the assumption that we must choose between seeing and believing, as if you can't have one if you have the other. In fact, if what we believe is true, then what we experience *should* line up with what we believe most of the time. As we will learn shortly, however, our limited senses can take us only so far.

Eventually, each and every person must trust in what he or she cannot see in order to live any story at all.

MY FAITH STORY

Just so you know, I am not an expert FaithWalker who's finally reached the destination. Not even close. But I have chosen to be intentional about making the journey to live a story worth telling. I've taken risks, and I've gotten to know many others who've done the same. My hope is to come alongside you as a fellow traveler and invite you to join us in the adventure.

It wasn't so very long ago that, if you had asked, I would have told you that I was indeed living a story worth telling. And I wouldn't have been all wrong. Raised in a Christian home by loving parents, I had served in the church my entire life, even as an elder and pastor. I had helped launch and lead a thriving Christian college-prep school for a dozen years. In that role, I had counseled thousands of students and parents on how to live lives of meaning, significance, and faith. And I was blessed with a wonderful wife and six awesome children.

To all appearances, I was living an exciting story. We had a comfortable house with beautiful gardens. We were a tight-knit family who took regular trips to Walt Disney World. I had a safe, secure job with benefits, not the least of which was nearly unlimited hugs from precious children and the very latest artwork from the kindergarten class. Best of all, I knew I was making a real difference in the world through ministry.

Yet I sensed a restlessness within myself, an awareness that I had quietly begun to drift into simply existing. And I suspected I'd allowed some God-given gifts to lie dormant. You see, for as long as I can recall, I have loved to write. Not just as an enjoyable pastime, but as something I was created to do. To put it in terms of the classic film *Chariots of Fire*, I had always sensed that when I wrote, I felt God's pleasure. The final clarifying words of my life purpose statement were these: "To get out of the boat. To write. To live. To die." Clearly I saw writing as basic to living, yet I always ended up shelving it in favor of other activities. Not bad things, just easier ones.

I believed God had given me a gift and a passion for communicating his truths to his people. I also believed that he expected me to use those gifts—and I was not, not fully anyway. For many years I tried to lead a school and write, while being a husband and being a father to six children. Maybe some can pull that off, but it never worked for me. It only made the situation more challenging. I had no shortage of sincere people thanking me for the work I was doing, telling me how essential I was to the ministry. I suppose at some level, I'd convinced myself that I was irreplaceable—and that's why I couldn't use *all* the gifts God had placed within me.

Sensing something stirring within, I enlisted a life coach, Dick Savidge, as a guide. I sought advice from wise counselors and then headed to a chilly lakeside cabin one spring afternoon to pray, think, and make some hard choices. It was only after a full day and night of wrestling with the options before me that the moment finally arrived: I realized I could not stay where I was and get where I longed to go. If my life were to become a story worth telling someday, I would have to act. In one of the most agonizing decisions of my life, I let go of the perceived security I found in my identity as a successful Christian ministry leader and committed to putting my gifts to work for God's kingdom at large. My friend Brad Lomenick, who knows quite a bit himself about stepping into the unknown, puts it like this: "Moving forward requires great risk, but the possibility of running away somehow feels more perilous."

I confess that I had very little idea what this new direction would mean, for me, for my family, and for my faith. I stepped away from the school and into the unknown like Abraham of old, bringing along six young children and a wife crazy enough to love me no matter what. And make no mistake, if I had known how difficult the journey was going to be, I might not have begun it at all. But sometimes ignorance is a blessing, because the rewards have also far exceeded anything I could have imagined.

To make a long story very short, we survived the next year with virtually no income, sold the comfortable house where we had planned to live for decades, and moved a thousand miles away—by faith. And God did all he promised to do and then some. I'll share more of my story and the lessons we learned as we take our journey together, but suffice it to say that it's a story that continues to require abundant faith. It's finally a story worth telling—and it's only just getting started.

THE GREATEST RISK YOU FACE

I don't know what you're confronting in life right now. Maybe you are torn between options—some seem right but scary, and some look a lot like drifting yet feel safe. Maybe the choice you are facing scares you to death. As we prepare to start up this trail together, consider these questions:

- What if the greatest risk you face is of a story left unlived?

- What if true security comes not from what you can see, but what you can't see?

- And what if your story becomes worth telling not for the bruises you avoid but for the giants you face—and defeat?

In the midst of my stepping out by faith to follow God's call on my life, I sensed his leading to partner with Equip Leadership (a ministry founded by John C. Maxwell) to train leaders in—of all places—Guam. A tropical island paradise in the South Pacific, Guam is a destination for sun, fun, and natural beauty as well as a key base for the United States military in that part of the world. It is also where one man I met had begun the journey to live a story worth telling long before I arrived.

Jon Pineda hadn't planned to make Guam his home until two executives from the company for which he worked in the Philippines just happened to sit next to one another on a flight to the island. By the time the flight was over, the fast-rising Jon was about to be promoted yet again, this time with a move to Guam. Such are the apparent coincidences that direct the life of every FaithWalker. But the accounting job that brought Jon and his young wife, Eva, to Guam in the early 1970s wasn't what would make their story a great one. No, for that they would need abundant faith.

After a rapid climb up the corporate ladder, Jon launched a real estate brokerage through which he soon achieved tremendous financial success. He and Eva and their two young boys were living the comfortable, upwardly mobile life with multiple homes and two Cadillacs—until Jon sensed a call from God to follow a very different path. He walked away from an extremely productive business to pastor a small group of Christians in Guam. His decision confused his extended family, who could not reconcile how he could walk away from financial success into a life of little to no income.

As Jon and Eva Pineda pressed forward, their bank accounts dwindled. They sold their houses, one by one, to pay the bills; when the money was gone, they persevered. Their son Paul recalls now how one week, all they had to eat was brussel sprouts. To this day, he doesn't eat them, though he is the first to testify to how God provided for his parents again and again on their walk of faith. And slowly but steadily, the church began to grow.

Soon they opened a Christian school in Guam that is still thriving to this day. Jon and Eva could have made it their goal to build a megachurch on the island. Instead, they began training other leaders to leave and start churches of their own. After four decades of the Pineda's ministry, well over one hundred thriving churches now exist all across the islands of Oceana as a direct result of their leadership.

In their present season of life, Jon and Eva's pace has slowed as they continue to serve faithfully but have handed leadership of the church and school to their son Paul. He continues their example, ministering to pastors and leaders everywhere from South Korea to Fiji to the Philippines—wherever God provides an opening.

In spite of the rich legacy of his parents' faith, what has made the most lasting impression on Paul is how his parents have demonstrated God's unconditional love in their own family. After his brother's marriage ended suddenly and painfully, his parents continued to love not only their own son and grandson, but their former daughter-in-law as well. Several years later, when she walked away from her second husband and their two children, Jon and Eva did what most would think unthinkable. They welcomed her second husband and the two children into their own family. And they continued to love their daughter-in-law, in spite of her struggles. Today, their demonstration of God's forgiveness and unfailing grace is bearing fruit, as she now worships alongside them all in the church founded by Jon and Eva, abundant proof that the unimaginable is possible when you live a story worth telling.

You don't even have to be a follower of Christ to appreciate the courage and perseverance required by Jon and Eva to live and love by faith. As I've gotten to know the Pinedas, along with many of the people they've influenced, I've been blown away by their authentic joy, genuine satisfaction with life, and a peace that comes from having lived a life of lasting purpose. But imagine if Jon had failed to realize that the greatest risk he faced was not stepping away from financial wealth but missing out on a story overflowing with abundant faith! He chose his own story. And so can you. Start now by exploring the trail ahead and reconnect with the dreams that might cause your story to become one worth telling.

EXPLORE THE TRAIL AHEAD

Prepare to embark on a journey to live a story worth telling.

- I mentioned a few characters from popular films and stories. Think of the people or characters whose life stories inspire you. Jot down their names and a few thoughts on why their stories resonate so deeply. Now imagine if your story could become one that inspires others to live a story worth telling.

- What dreams did you once have that are now faded, or what promptings to step out have you ignored? Give yourself permission to name them now. You cannot go back to change the past, nor does it help to live in regret, but some dreams can and should be reawakened.

- What might you dare to attempt if fear no longer held you back? If money were no object? If you had ample time to pursue it? Write it down, then ask yourself this: at the end of my life, will my excuses for not attempting this dream be satisfying?

- Sometimes the most fulfilling dreams are right in front of us every day through relationships with the people closest to us. Think of the opportunities you have to shape the future right now! What three practical things can you do this week to live a story that is less about you and more about creating a legacy?

- I enlisted a life coach as a guide for my journey. Whom might you invite to join in the journey ahead as a trusted advisor? Be careful to choose someone who aligns with your beliefs and who has already demonstrated a willingness to live courageously.

Faith Finds a Focus

D ad, they even have a real treasure map!" It was a sunny evening in suburban Ohio when my kids excitedly presented their report. They had stopped a preschooler and a toddler strolling by our house and discovered that the girl, age four, and her younger brother, age two, were on an expedition, complete with a map to guide them in their quest.

My children thought the kids' adventure was cool. But my daddy-senses began tingling immediately. The street on which we lived was a busy state route, one where most drivers ignore the posted speed of 35 mph. Not the safest place for unsupervised kids to take a stroll. So I decided it was time for action. I did what any decent father would do. I asked my seven-year-old daughter to come along for support and began tracking the two juvenile explorers down the sidewalk.

They were making surprisingly good time as they unwittingly crossed through intersections, oblivious to the cars and drivers who alertly paused to let them pass. I didn't want to alarm them if they were to notice a six-foot-four guy in wild pursuit, so I hatched an ingenious plan. We would come alongside them as if we were fellow treasure seekers! With any luck, I thought, we could persuade them to alter their course—you know, back to civilization. Or something. (It was the best I could do without my wife's help.)

When we finally caught up, we found they were indeed on a hunt for hidden treasure. This brave duo, clearly led by the very determined four-year-old, had made it their aim to find the treasure before nightfall. When they learned that we were on a similar expedition, they happily showed us their map of "Pirate Country" and "Lake Marraba" (which looked surprisingly similar to Florida and Lake Okeechobee to me, but then I'm not well versed in the ways of pirates). I agreed that finding the treasure was, of course, a top priority. Thinking quickly, I warned them to consider the monsters that might be guarding it. I thought that ploy would definitely scare them into returning. But the two-year-old promptly scolded me, "There's no such thing as monsters." Duh. What was I thinking?

Not to be outdone by a two-year-old, I took a different approach. "Well, that's true. But it's almost nighttime. I wonder if we should turn back from our expedition for now and set out again in the morning when it's not dark." That did it. The brave girl's eyes widened. She quickly instructed her brother that it was indeed time to find shelter for the night. We promptly turned toward home.

As we walked back, a frantic mother in sleepwear came running toward us, robe flapping behind as her arms flailed wildly. The two treasure-seekers had apparently escaped unnoticed from a backyard when Mom dozed off. The relieved mother said the usual stuff we loving parents say in such circumstances: "How could you do this to me? You're grounded until you die!" The two adventurers just looked at her as if she were crazy. What was she worried about? After all, they had a map.

What they did not have was even the slightest awareness of the danger they had been in. They didn't recognize the care of the drivers who braked to let them pass safely. They didn't know they had been under the watchful eye of a guardian who intervened as night descended around them. The one thing they finally did fear was darkness, which couldn't harm them at all. From their perspective, they were on their way to treasure.

What struck me then was how much they took for granted, how much they took by faith. But the focus of their faith—a tourist map of Florida, as it turned out—was incapable of taking them where they wanted to go. Their story was well on its way to becoming a tragedy on the nightly news, because where we focus our faith matters.

CHECK YOUR COORDINATES

- Do you sometimes feel like those children who thought they knew where they were going but really didn't have a clue? Why?

- Who or what would you say is the primary focus of your faith?

- Could someone tell the focus of your faith by the actions that you take?

TRUST REQUIRES AN OBJECT

When it comes to living a story worth telling, each of us is no different from those sincere but misguided children. Each one of us lives life by faith in something, even if we aren't always consciously aware of what that something may be. That's just how faith works.

In the previous chapter, I defined faith in this way: *faith is doing what you believe to be true, often in spite of what you see, sense, or feel.* Astute readers will note this definition of faith is a broad one, applicable not just to those who claim to be people of faith. The reality is that each of our stories is written by our faith. We all trust in what we believe to be true and then do something because of that belief. We live our stories based on the focus of that trust, often in spite of what we see, sense, or feel, because trust needs an object.

I know some of you may groan at the thought of anything resembling grammar class, but bear with me for a moment. Verbs such as *trust* (they're called *transitive verbs* if you want to feel really smart) transfer something from one subject to another. Thus the action must be followed by an object to make any sense. For example, a transitive verb like *put* must be followed by whatever it is you are putting. "I put" makes no sense, but "I put my shoes on the floor" does. The object *shoes* becomes the focus of the putting as I transfer action to them.

Love is another transitive verb. Imagine if I gave a Valentine's Day card to my wife that read simply, "I love." Her puzzled response would likely be, "You love—what? Who? And it had better be me!" Why? Because we innately recognize that love requires an object. I must transfer my affection to someone or something or it isn't love. Love can't exist without a focus.

So it is with faith. When we say we have faith, that we trust or believe, the next necessary question is—*in what* do we believe? Or *in whom* do we trust? If we talk about having faith without a focus, we're not talking about faith at all, but irrational silliness. Just saying "I believe" doesn't cut it. You see, faith demands a focus in order to exist in the same way love requires an object for affection.

OUR INESCAPABLE NEED TO TRUST

Every time we board an airplane we set the focus of our faith on the pilots, the crew, the airline, and the maintenance staff—none of whom we've ever met. Usually that faith proves to be well placed. You may recall the miraculous landing made several years ago by Captain Sullenberger, a US Air pilot. After both engines were disabled when the plane struck a flock of geese shortly after takeoff, he landed safely on the frigid waters of the Hudson River—and all on board survived.

But it wasn't just the pilot who came through. Someone (let's call him Joe) inspected the seat belts when they were manufactured and slapped his "Inspected by #264" sticker on them. When the plane finally stopped on the murky Hudson, the emergency escape chutes opened by the doors and began to double as life rafts—just as someone (maybe Marge in Omaha) designed them to do. The survivors will never know every person involved in saving their lives that day, but they put their faith in them when they boarded that plane.

We have to trust people for just about every activity in life. We trust in a lonely soldier on night duty at a nuclear missile silo in North Dakota, a police officer fresh out of the academy, and a nurse monitoring an IV drip on the night shift. We trust the lineman climbing the utility pole in the middle of a blizzard, the driver about to stop at the next intersection, and the kindergarten teacher supervising a bathroom break for our child. And those are but a few examples of the thousands of people we trust just to survive each day.

We also trust in the laws of nature with little thought. We wake each day expecting gravity to function in the same way it did yesterday. We depend on friction to bring our car to a halt or to let us simply walk across the room. We make plans as if the sun will rise tomorrow even though we have no say in how our solar system operates. We flick a switch and expect the laws that govern electrical charges to keep our mobile devices ready to use. You get the picture. Faith is everywhere.

Without faith, without trusting in what we believe to be true in spite of what we see, sense, or feel, life comes to a screeching halt. When it comes right down to it, we are all "people of faith," even the most devout atheists. Where the Christ-follower believes in the supernatural revelation of truth by an infinite Creator, the atheist believes in his own assessment of the nature of reality and the impossibility that God could exist and reveal himself in various ways. The professing atheist cannot prove that there is no God based on what he or she sees, senses, and feels, but he or she acts *as if* this belief were true. The atheist walks by faith just as a Christian does, but with a radically different focus.

Even those who say there is no truth by which we can define value or worth must live as if they believe otherwise. As the French philosopher Voltaire famously said, "If God did not exist, it would be necessary to invent him" to make sense of the universe. Perhaps faith in the unseen is essential to existing in this universe because an unseen Creator designed it to be so. Perhaps this same Creator designed us to interact with his universe by living a life saturated with faith. Prominent MIT researcher Marvin Minsky describes the atheist's dilemma this way: "The physical world provides no room for freedom of the will [that is, truth beyond our senses. And yet] we're virtually forced to maintain that belief, even though we know it's false." So although a secularist like Minsky believes there is no room for faith, he must live by faith to make sense of living in a world where faith is impossible. Sounds like a lot of faith to me, just wrongly focused.

IT MATTERS WHAT TRAIN YOU GET ON

The Polar Express (2004) is a masterpiece of modern filmmaking based on a children's book by Chris Van Allsburg. It has quickly become an annual holiday stalwart for our family and millions of others around the world. But it has also become the model for popular thinking about faith that is dangerously misleading for those seeking to live a story worth telling. In spite of the warm, fuzzy feelings the film produces while taking children to the North Pole and back, the overarching message is one of indifference to the focus of faith. Even the theme song "Believe," sung by the talented Josh Groban, ends by repeating the refrain "If you just believe" with little concern for what the focus of that belief should be. Near the end of the film, the train conductor drives home the central lesson that the young boy should take from his magical experience: "The thing about trains...it doesn't matter where they're going. What matters is deciding to get on."

Thus the core message of the fable is this: *what* you believe is not as important as the fact *that* you do believe in something—Santa Claus, for example. But as we've already seen, faith without a focus is not faith at all. "Just believe" just isn't good enough. In this thinking, what defines your story is the power you exercise in making your choice. In the real world, there is a vast difference between believing it is your mission to bring death to the infidels in Afghanistan and believing it is your mission to sacrificially serve orphans in the slums of Calcutta. It does matter what train you get on.

This popular form of existential thinking has infiltrated Western culture. According to it, when we exercise autonomy by making a choice, we define who we are as masters of our fate and captains of our souls. Simply by following our own hearts to make our own choices, we live stories worth telling. Such shallow thinking considers nearly all destinations equally valid provided you choose to get on a train. As long as it's your choice, anything goes.

The thing about trains, however, is that they all go somewhere. Each moves along the rails from one station to another, in a specific direction and to a specific place. To say that it doesn't matter what train we get on is nonsense. Tell that to the millions of Jews who were forced to board trains for Nazi concentration camps during World War II.

By choosing the focus of your faith, you set the direction for your story. If you don't like the direction of your story, change the focus of your faith. When people who lack a focus for their faith are bombarded with confusing calls to pick a direction, any direction, many simply throw up their hands. Overwhelmed, they choose to drift like soap bubbles. Maybe we think that if we don't actively seek to live a story worth telling, we can't be held responsible for failing to do so. But refusing to make a choice is in itself a choice to surrender control of our stories to someone else. Our stories remain our own in spite of our best efforts to shift the responsibility to others.

Despite what some might say, faith is not getting on whatever train happens to come along. Nor is it a blind leap into the unknown. It does not require you to check your brain at the door. Such a view has been popularized by Eastern mystic films such as the classic *Star Wars*, which has defined movie storytelling for nearly four decades. In it, the young hero Luke Skywalker must ignore his instruments, close his eyes, and fire blindly into the Death Star. To succeed, Luke must stop thinking and start believing, as if the two cannot coexist. The lesson of such films is that thinking and believing are necessarily at odds.

But the adventure of living a life of abundant faith is not some crazy leap into an unknown canyon, nor is it at odds with our intellect. It does not mean that you stop thinking; it means you become more aware of what you *do* believe. It means you live more intentionally based on what you believe to be true, even if what you see doesn't quite line up. Even if it frightens you. This is the kind of authentic faith that shapes the universe and that can transform your story into one worth telling. You do need to choose a train or you will have one chosen for you, and it matters greatly what train you're on.

 ## Prepare Your Gear

Three Ways to Find the Faith Connection

We're not all philosophers and theologians. But here are a few proven exercises to figure out where our beliefs can—or should—take us:

1. **Why?** All too often we accept the status quo in life without asking *why*. When you say, "I believe_____," be willing to ask the next tough question—why? When you get an answer, ask *why* again and repeat until you identify whom or what you truly trust.

2. **So what?** If I believe _____, *so what*? What are the implications for my life, my family, and my community? How will it influence the story I am living?

3. **If..., then....** Try completing this statement about something you believe: If I believe _____, then _____. For example, *if I believe* I should build a relationship with my child, *then* I should schedule time to invest in his or her life this week. Or *if I believe* my dream is worth pursuing, *then* I should take the next step to fulfill it.

THE FOCUS THAT MAKES YOUR STORY WORTH TELLING

When it comes to the focus of our faith, there appears to be a host of options out there. We can trust in the government, a religion, our income, or any number of things. But when you get right down to it, most are manifestations of only three options: yourself, others, or God.

Yourself

When you are the focus of your faith, you rely ultimately on your own understanding to guide your story. That's not to say you don't consult others, but you depend on your own conclusions, usually what you can see, sense, or feel, as the ultimate authority for making sense of the universe and your place in it. You may even believe a god exists, but it is a small god who must conform to your story if that god wants the privilege of being included in your story. We see this thinking displayed by celebrities receiving awards as they say, "I first want to thank God" before accepting awards for performances inconsistent with what God has said is pleasing to him. But we also see it creeping in every day in each of our own lives when our first thought is not *How does God view this?* but *How will this affect my own comfort and lifestyle?*

Others

When you focus your faith on others, you are acknowledging that you are not qualified to exercise ultimate authority in this universal tale. Yet you think someone, or a collection of someones, just might be. So you trust in the opinions of other people you deem more qualified than yourself. You may trust in the opinions of great thinkers, artists, leaders, scientists, or even theologians.

In its most destructive form, this thinking may cause you to permit a specific individual to dictate your story, even if that relationship proves harmful to your physical and emotional well-being. Basically, this option is the same as the first (self-focused) in that you are still the ultimate authority for determining *whose* opinions matter in the universe. The only difference is that you pass along responsibility for the details to others. At the end of the day, your trust still focuses on people, just like yourself, who have flaws and limited understanding.

Adding more people with such defects does not ultimately make the focus more reliable, nor does it shift responsibility for your story to anyone else.

God

When I refer to *God* here, I am not referring to glorified humans, like the ancient Greek concept of the divine, where a whimsical and unpredictable Zeus hurls lightning bolts from on high. Nor do I mean a vague spiritual force that animates all living things. I also don't mean a meek, heavenly being who always speaks in hushed tones, wears an iconic halo, and carries a harp.

I am talking about the self-existent One, the God who is and who is not silent. God needs neither anyone nor anything in order to be, yet God chose to create all things, including us, to craft a story worth telling, a story that would become the standard for measuring every other story. This God did not leave us to wonder about him, but revealed himself to us personally, indirectly through what he created and directly through the written word that we now call the Old and New Testaments. But he didn't stop there. As evidence of his infinite genius, he introduced a plot twist: He became one of us in order to restore the relationship that had been shattered by our lack of faith in him. The Creator became part of his creation; the Master of all became a humble servant, in order to reconcile his enemies to himself. By his sacrifice, we find new life—by faith. He became the hero that each of our stories desperately needs. And now he invites us to align our story with his.

In the chapters to come, we'll explore together why a focus on God is the most empowering and how you can choose to live a story worth telling because of it. We find our greatest fulfillment when we align our story with God's story through a life of ongoing, authentic faith. Just because we think our map leads us to treasure doesn't mean that it will. And just because we're on a train, doesn't mean it will take us to a story worth telling. Take a moment now to consider the current focus of your faith and how that might affect the course of your life story.

Explore the Trail Ahead

Get clear on your faith focus with these simple exercises:

- Have you ever put your faith in someone who led you off course? Did anything change if you believed in him or her with more passion? Why doesn't sincerity or good intentions matter if you are on the wrong train?

- Examine your life to determine where you look for ultimate authority. Do you tend to trust in yourself, something other than yourself, or God? Choose a few different areas of your life (money, relationships, calling, recreation, etc.) and identify specific evidence to support your conclusions.

- On a scale of 1 to 10, with 1 being the least and 10 the most, rank how intentional you have been about living according to what you believe. Now do the same for how intentional you want to become. The difference between the two represents an opportunity for growth and a goal to aspire to as we continue this journey.

- If you already embrace God as your ultimate authority and the focus of your faith, imagine you recently reconnected with an old friend who asked, "So why do you trust in God to make your story worth telling?" Write a brief response answering that question.

3

FAITH MAKES YOUR STORY WORTH TELLING

At the time of Jesus' ministry on earth, the people of northern Galilee awoke one morning with a puzzle to solve. Over the last several days, they had seen Jesus heal the sick throughout the area. An excited crowd of about twenty thousand had gathered, hoping to see more cool tricks. They had not been disappointed. Jesus fed the massive crowd using a lunch of five loaves and two fish offered by a young boy. Without a Walmart or Piggly Wiggly, Jesus conjured up food that would cost tens of thousands of dollars in today's economy. The people had settled in for the night wondering what amazing feat this Jesus fellow might do the next morning.

But when they awoke, Jesus was gone—and with him, their hopes for an encore performance. But where did Jesus go? And even more puzzling, how did he get there undetected? News soon arrived that answered their first question: Jesus was once again healing and helping on the opposite side of the sea, in the region of Gennesaret. Thoroughly surprised by this revelation, they set out in boats to track Jesus down and demand an explanation.

As they sailed, no doubt they talked through their dilemma. They had seen Jesus' disciples set off in a boat the night before *without* Jesus. They had, no doubt, seen the fierce storm that arose during the night, making any additional travel impossible. Besides, all other boats were accounted for. They put two and two together, and they didn't get four. And yet, sure enough, when they reached Gennesaret, there was Jesus. So they began to question him in a way that revealed their own hearts: "Rabbi, when did you get here?" (John 6:25).

Note that they did not ask *how* he got there, only *when*. Why? It's possible their question reflects a passion for punctuality. Far more likely, they thought if they could just get all the facts, they'd figure out how he'd pulled this one off. But Jesus correctly identified the issue as a lack of faith. They were struggling to believe the truth revealed right in front of them. They saw the evidence that he was who he claimed to be, and yet they sought an explanation they could reproduce on their own, apart from divine intervention.

His response was essentially this: *Why are you looking for me in the first place? Because I did amazing tricks? Don't look for temporary bread from the Son of Man* (see John 6:26-27). Jesus challenged their motives and reasserted his claim to be God. They had just seen him perform many miraculous works, not counting this inexplicable journey from one side of the sea to the other, for which there was no natural explanation. Yet they continued to question him: "What shall we do, that we may work the works of God?" (John 6:28 NKJV).

The frustrating fact that they had just witnessed the works of God and still did not respond in faith is what moved Jesus to make this stunning statement: "This is the work of God, that you believe in Him whom He sent" (v. 29 NKJV). Most important here is what Jesus did *not* say, such as, "Now folks, if you look to your left, you'll be able to see one of the many wonderful works of God." Instead he identified what he said was *the* mightiest work of God—faith. And not just any faith, but faith focused on him.

The mightiest work of God—greater than miraculous feedings and midnight water-walking—is that we who had totally rejected him would now fully trust him. Altering the weather and the laws of physics is impressive, but pretty straightforward for an omnipotent God. Matter and energy simply obey their Creator. Water can't resist the will of the Almighty. Wind doesn't have a mind corrupted by sin. We do. That is why God's greatest work is transforming a heart from its default position of unbelief to belief, from faith in ourselves to faith in him—and to do so without coercing or violating our will.

When we who were his enemies, who were without strength, who not only had no desire but also no capacity to love him—when we freely trust him, there can be only one explanation: God did that. Our faith becomes evidence of God working the impossible within us. We could say then that the mightiest work of God is to change the focus of our faith from *me* to *he*.

THE GIFT WE CHOOSE TO IGNORE

As we've seen, faith in God is a gift. It isn't something you can conjure up within yourself or muster the strength to embrace. No one can persuade you to focus your faith in the God who has revealed himself to us through the written word and in the person of Jesus. As the Apostle Paul said in his letter to the Ephesians, "For it is by grace you have been saved, through faith—and this not from yourselves, it is the gift of God—not by works, so that no one can boast. For we are God's handiwork" (2:8-10 NIV). When our hearts awaken to trust in him, it's because he has done his gracious work of faith in us.

Having our faith supernaturally refocused on God changes everything. When God begins this work of faith in us, we turn from trusting in ourselves to trusting in him. His work dramatically shifts our entire life orientation. But that's not the end of the story. In fact, it's merely the beginning. For faith to be faith, we must do something because of it. We must live it out.

Imagine that the current chairman of Disney, Michael Iger, wrote you a letter. In it, he gave you a ticket to any and all of the Disney parks worldwide—for free. Maybe before that you couldn't afford even a one-day ticket. But this kind of access couldn't be purchased. It could only be given to you. Best of all, it would never expire. Most of us would think that was pretty cool.

But then imagine that the pass didn't just get you into the parks, it got you onto any ride or into any attraction any time you wanted—with no lines and no waiting. To sweeten the deal, you could eat any food, anytime, anyplace without reservations. Just walk in and you'd be seated immediately to enjoy the best meals—no charge.

As if that weren't enough, what if Iger wrote in his letter that Disney no longer thought of you as a guest, but as family? He invited you to become part of the Disney creative team in whatever way your strengths and passions led you, to help create new guest experiences or design new rides and attractions. In short, he offered to empower your own creative energy with an unlimited budget to do whatever you love to do in advancing the vision of the company. And just for good measure, you would have a suite in the castle at the Magic Kingdom with a standing offer to live there whenever you wanted. How good a gift would that be?

But now imagine that in spite of this almost unimaginable generosity, you choose not to take advantage of it. You rarely visit any of the parks. And when you do, you stand in line with everyone else. You pack peanut butter and jelly sandwiches instead of dining at five-star restaurants. You stay at a hotel more than an hour away. Consequently, you come home more exhausted than when you go, so you don't even enjoy it. Instead, you settle for living somewhere you don't really like, working at a job you hate but pays the bills, and spending all your spare time trying to recover from the stress. But—as you make sure to tell everyone—you *do* have an all-access pass to the happiest place on earth.

How feeble would it be for you to have access to such abundance and so rarely use it? Pause for a moment to consider to what extent your life presently reflects abundant faith in God's promises.

 ## CHECK YOUR COORDINATES

- Do you think of the faith within you as the mightiest work of God? Why or why not?

- Does your current walk of faith more fully reveal God's majesty? If not, how can you change that?

- Do you make life choices based on your trust in God's promises to you? If not, why? How can you practice more faith?

SHATTERING THE SALVATION BOX

Most of us settle for a story full of peanut butter and jelly sandwiches and deep frustration while ignoring the gift that yields meaning and lasting satisfaction. Ironically, we Christ-followers, who are supposedly all about faith, are as guilty of this as anyone else. Even though we've been given an all-access pass to live lives of abundant faith, we don't. We seldom act on the gift of faith we've so graciously been given, but that doesn't stop us from telling others how blessed we are to have received it. Our faith lies dormant, tossed casually aside, to be mentioned only in holy, hushed tones on Sundays or when a crisis reminds us we need it to breathe.

The irony is that we call ourselves "people of the Book," a Book replete with stories of abundant faith, yet we wince at the thought of living a story of our own. We applaud the tale of Joseph and his journey to become Grand Vizier of Egypt, but we run from any possibility of doing time in a royal prison to gain influence for God. We cheer on Moses as he answers the call to leave behind the comfortable family life of a shepherd to lead God's people to freedom, yet we let our own callings slip away in favor of the perceived security of a suburban castle, health care benefits, and a hefty 401(k). We might even snicker at Peter's frantic cries as he slips beneath the waves while we dig our own fingernails deeper into our WWJD life preservers, never daring to step out of the boat ourselves.

Some fixate on a single conversion experience as though that were the whole story, but faith is not so much an event as a process. The Apostle Paul explained this truth using the familiar language of an ongoing journey: "We walk by faith, not by sight" (2 Corinthians 5:7 NKJV).

Walking by faith to live a story worth telling involves traveling from Point A to Point B. It is an ongoing process in which we actively participate, cultivating our faith in God and enjoying its benefits in ever-deepening relationship with him. All too often we think that once we've received the gift of saving faith, our story will write itself. We recognize that God begins the work within us, yet we fail to see how essential our ongoing faith is to being "conformed to the image of his Son" (Romans 8:29). This journey of faith God has begun in us is about shaping us to do something so great that we struggle even to imagine it.

By labeling faith as essential only at the initial restoration of our relationship with God, we confine faith to what I call the *Salvation Box*. It isn't a literal box. You won't find one in your local Christian bookstore alongside a pack of Testamints. But we confine our faith to the Salvation Box nonetheless. We think of faith as how we "got saved" or "stepped across the line" but give little thought to how it should alter the daily trajectory of our story. We seldom think of faith as necessary for surviving every moment of every day. When the going gets tough, we reach in the box, grab a handful of stale faith, and toss a cloud of hurried prayer—like pixie dust—into the air above us.

Confining the mightiest work of God to the Salvation Box won't do. Many Christians think that once God saves them by faith they should be able to coast. The problem with coasting is this: heaven is not downhill. That would be the other destination. *Faith* must write our entire story—or none at all. The Apostle Paul described this stark reality in sobering terms: "I have been crucified with Christ and I no longer live, but Christ lives in me. And the life that I now live in my body, I live by faith, indeed, by the faithfulness of God's Son, who loved me and gave himself for me" (Galatians 2:20).

When Paul said that he had been crucified with Christ, he eliminated all options *except* that of living a life guided wholly by his faith in God. What he believed about the generous love of God then determined how he lived every detail of his story. If he had been only partly alive to faith, he'd still have been mostly dead.

Perhaps you've seen the scene from the cult movie classic, *The Princess Bride.* When Inigo the Spaniard asks the eccentric Miracle Max to revive brave Westley, we get the following bizarre exchange:

Inigo: He's dead. He can't talk.

Miracle Max: Hoo hoo hoo! Look who knows so much, heh? Well, it just so happens that your friend here is only mostly dead. There's a big difference between mostly dead and all dead. Please, open his mouth. [Puts the bellows to Westley's mouth, and blows air in.] Now, mostly dead is slightly alive. Now, all dead…well, with all dead, there's usually only one thing that you can do.

Inigo: What's that?

Miracle Max: Go through his clothes and look for loose change.

Too many of us settle for roaming the world like Westley, hovering somewhere between mostly dead and partly alive. We're not fully alive to Christ with a faith that impacts all of life, but we're not exactly dead. You can't keep us from church on Sunday, but we can't explain why church matters on Monday. We know we should trust God, so we lean that direction outwardly while inwardly hedging our bets, just in case God doesn't come through as promised.

The result is that many of us have the appearance of faith, but not the power. About all we can do is go through our Sunday best and look for church bulletins to recycle. We're walking all right, but not by faith. We're in constant motion but going nowhere that matters. God has called us to strike out on a grand adventure of faith, but we've chosen to look busy on a treadmill of pious activity.

On the Treadmills at God's Gym

You can actually work up quite a sweat on treadmills at the gym. In fact, up close it's hard to tell the difference between someone in the gym and someone out on the trail. It's only when you step back and look at the big picture that you can see the progress—or the lack thereof. Maybe that's why we like the treadmill so much. As long as no one examines our lives too closely, we appear to be full of faith. We get all the affirmation from the other fake-walkers huffing away around us and little of the discomfort of true adventure into the unknown. As long as nobody rocks the boat or asks too many questions, the illusion of faith continues.

When I first publicly shared with others that I believed God was calling me to step out by faith, I heard comments like, "We'll pray for you. But of course, God doesn't call everyone to do such things." Some even cautioned others not to be too hasty in following my example: "That walk is not for everyone." Which walk exactly? The one that insists on living all of life by faith in the One who loved me and gave himself for me, no matter where that may take me? I'd say that walk is for every Christian.

When God called Abram, we're told he "went out without knowing where he was going" (Hebrews 11:8). It's just too easy to dismiss that call to step into the unknown as the exception to the rule. God calls us far more often than we'd like to admit to walk by faith in a way that seems foolish to the rest of world and even to the church. We forget that God "chose what the world considers weak to shame the strong" (1 Corinthians 1:27). So we turn up the GodTunes and tune out God's call. We step up the pace of our treadmill lives to justify why we refuse to leave the gym and hit the trail.

If you choose to live a faithless life, you'll get plenty of encouragement in the Christian gym. No one wants to be the only one awkwardly but energetically speeding along on the treadmill. Few of us are willing, like the child from the tale of the naked emperor, to shatter the illusion by looking at ourselves and stating the obvious: "This Christian has no faith!"

When we settle for a treadmill life, we choose what we believe to be the "safe and secure" option. Yet we feel the consequences of that faithless decision deep within our souls. In spite of our pious exterior, we don't like it—not one bit. For as A. G. Buckham poignantly warns, "Monotony is the awful reward of the careful."

 ## PREPARE YOUR GEAR

How to Shatter the Salvation Box—and Set Your Faith Free

1. Stop thinking salvation is all about you. Yes, God loves you. And seven billion other people. He has bigger plans than selling you fire insurance. Get ready for the adventure ahead!

2. Recognize that God's plan isn't primarily about getting you *out* of this world, but getting his love back *into* his world—*through* you!

3. Quit coasting. God began a work in you to shake the foundations of the forces of darkness. Which ones are trembling because of the story you are living now?

4. Guard against busyness becoming a replacement for a transformed life. Many of us are busy in the gym because we're afraid to take our faith out into the field.

5. Stand on the shoulders of other FaithWalkers to apply gospel truth to every area of life. One of the best-written resources for this big-picture perspective is *Total Truth: Liberating Christianity from Its Cultural Captivity* by Nancy Pearcey (Wheaton, IL: Crossway, 2004).

REVEALING THE MAJESTY OF GOD

In addition to how unfulfilling it must be to live such an uninspired story, there's one rather significant problem for the Christ-follower who does not fully depend on faith: "Everything that isn't based on faith is sin" (Romans 14:23).

Just before raising her brother, Lazarus, from the dead, Jesus reminded Martha, "If you believe, you will see God's glory" (John 11:40). Implied in his statement is that the opposite is equally true: if you don't believe, you will *not* see God's glory. It's not just that we miss out on miraculous feats or the next level of sainthood. We don't just fail to get our super-saint badge or the deed to a bigger mansion. It's more serious than that. When we fail to believe fully in Christ, to live out what we believe to be true about him, we fall short of fully revealing the glory of God.

Why should that be troubling? In his letter to the Romans, the Apostle Paul defined the essence of sin as to "fall short of God's glory" (3:23). This is why Paul stated with such authority that "everything that isn't based on faith is sin." Our faithlessness conceals the glory of God both from us and from a hurting world around us, for it frustrates the very purpose for which we were created. When we place great faith in our great God, we pull back the curtains to reveal more of his majesty. E. M. Bounds, one of my favorite authors, describes what happens when we fail to believe: "Great faith enables Christ to do great things....We have hedged God in till we have little faith in his power. We have conditioned the exercise of his power till we have a little God, and little faith in a little god."

God's mission is to fully glorify himself, to reveal his majesty for the benefit of all creation. As Jonathan Edwards famously preached, "God is glorified in the work of redemption in this, that there appears in it so absolute and universal a dependence of the redeemed on him." David Platt voices a similar thought in *Radical*, where he says, "This is how God works. He puts people in positions where they are desperate for His power, and then He shows his provision in ways that display his greatness."

THE MOST QUOTED VERSE IN THE BIBLE

When God speaks, you know the message is important. When he repeats himself, you'd better listen extra carefully. When God says it three times, you know it must be absolutely vital to his mission. But one statement in the Bible actually appears four times. As best I can tell, it is the most quoted verse in the Bible. One key verse from the book of Habakkuk is quoted three times in the New Testament and is essential to understanding the role of faith in living a story worth telling. It says, simply, "The righteous person will live by faith" (Romans 1:17).

If living a story worth telling is to be a grand adventure, then think of this verse as a homing beacon that continuously transmits vital directions reminding you *how* you can do it—by living all of life based on what we believe to be true, often in spite of what we see, sense, or feel.

But what does it mean to be "righteous"? The word refers to those who are in good standing, or right relationship, with God. Being righteous (some translations use "just") is all about being pleasing to God. And isn't that the essence of our calling?

As Paul wrote to the Corinthian believers, "Our goal is to be acceptable to Him" (2 Corinthians 5:9).

But God is equally clear that there can be no delighting him apart from abundant faith: "It's impossible to please God without faith" (Hebrews 11:6). Not just challenging, but *impossible*. "My righteous one will live by faith, and my whole being won't be pleased with anyone who shrinks back" (Hebrews 10:38). "Won't be pleased"—period. This is perhaps the most sobering statement of all: "I will hide My face from them, I will see what their end will be, for they are a perverse generation, children in whom is no faith" (Deuteronomy 32:20 NKJV). Walking on treadmills isn't going to cut it.

To be pleasing to God requires living with abundant faith focused on God. Here's the standard for determining whether your life is becoming a story worth telling or just a soap bubble preparing to pop: Will your story please God? One thing is clear: the only story God will find pleasing is one lived by ongoing faith in the Son of God who loved you and gave himself for you. The same Son of God who invites us to participate in his mightiest work so we can fully reveal his majesty to all. "It's impossible to please God without faith." But all things are possible for the one who truly lives by faith in him.

Once we've focused our faith in the right direction, we can start packing our hearts and minds for the journey. We begin by ensuring faith opens our eyes to see clearly the path to adventure that lies ahead.

Explore the Trail Ahead

- As we noted, "To be pleasing to God requires living with abundant faith focused on God." List some areas of your life where you know you are living with abundant faith in God. In what areas do you struggle to live with rich faith? Why?

- Have you seen the greatness of God displayed through someone else's faith? Briefly record the experience and its impact on you.

- Who looks to you for spiritual leadership? How might you show your faith in God to them? List their names and consider how you might help shape their futures by letting them see you walk with deeper faith in your great God.

- Have you fallen short in the past when you had the chance to trust? Have you ever discussed that failure with God? Take a moment now to ask his forgiveness and for the strength to get back up and walk by faith at the next opportunity.

- How busy are you? As you've read this chapter, you may have found yourself thinking, *This all sounds great, but I'm too busy living my life to figure out my story.* Even if what you are doing is good work, it may not be the best God has for you. Schedule a retreat, some time for you to get alone with God and listen, so he can realign your story with his.

4

FAITH OPENS YOUR EYES

Charles and Charla Pereau would have never dreamed of the story they would live by following God one step at a time. First came an unexpected request from a missionary. Would they consider adopting a Zapotec baby boy from Mexico? Three months later, they were cradling a tiny raven-haired boy, whom they took home to southern California to join their family.

But God's plan was only just getting started. As their love for their son grew, so did their concern for their neighbors south of the border. Five years later, Charles was asked to drive a truck of clothing to an orphanage in Tijuana, Mexico. Though the orphanage was just twenty-five miles south of San Diego, God would use the short journey to change their lives yet again. The orphanage overlooked a garbage dump where more than ninety abandoned children lived. The sight caused Charla to weep. The children living in the garbage looked just like her little boy at home.

They delivered the clothes and continued south into the Baja

Peninsula. They were lost and out of gas when they stumbled upon a group of crumbling adobe buildings. Images from the dump were fresh in Charla's mind, and her heart was still raw for those abandoned children. As she looked out over the arid land surrounding the old buildings, faith opened her eyes to what she describes as a God-given vision. She heard the sound of children's laughter in the empty structures. The desert plain became a field of wheat before her eyes. The words of John 4:35 reverberated through her: "Lo, the fields are white unto harvest."

Charla believed she had seen God's vision for that place. With little more than faith, she and Charles bought that land and started Foundation for His Ministry (FFHM). Through hard work they revamped the adobe buildings and started bringing in the little ones in from the streets. Forty-eight years later, they haven't stopped. The ministry now runs three orphanages throughout Mexico and has planted multiple churches and a Bible school for training church leaders.

When I visited the vibrant facility in Baja in 2008, I met Charla, who at the time of this writing is still involved in the ministry as much as possible. I held the joyful orphans rescued from the streets and garbage dumps. I saw firsthand the joyful FaithWalkers who care for the disabled and poor, provide free medical care, run a school, sustain a macadamia nut orchard, manage a fire and rescue department relied on by the community, and much more. Charla and Charles know that only God could have grown this work from a vision in one woman's mind to an organization that has influenced thousands. That's the kind of story he can write when you are willing to let faith open your eyes.

WHAT FAITH SHOWS US

Just north of our home in Atlanta, the Smoky Mountains begin to rise as part of the greater Appalachian Mountain range that runs along most of the eastern United States. From Georgia, they stretch northward between Tennessee and North Carolina, forming some of the most beautiful country in the world. But these mountains are called the Smokies for a reason. Due to vegetation that gives off certain chemicals, the mountains are known for their persistent patches of low-lying fog. The dense, drifting clouds make for picturesque scenes throughout the range, but they also make for some treacherous driving conditions. Road signs warn, "Watch for Dense Fog," and visibility can be close to zero at times. If you encounter the fog while hiking the Appalachian Trail, you're better off just sitting down and waiting to avoid pitching headlong over the edge of a cliff.

So it is with any journey we take. Unless we have a way to see clearly, we might as well be walking with our eyes closed. But faith opens our eyes. To live a story worth telling, you must first be able to see where you're going. But not just any sight will do. For as Paul said, "We walk by faith, *not* by sight" (2 Corinthians 5:7 NKJV, emphasis mine). What we see with our natural eyes can deceive us. When we look with eyes opened by abundant faith, then we can see—and do—what others deem impossible.

If you struggle to see with abundant faith, don't think yourself strange. At least your failures aren't recorded permanently in the pages of Scripture, as they were for one servant of the prophet Elisha. It seems Elisha had been frustrating the secret plans of the king of Syria. Every time the king would concoct a way to take over the world—starting with Israel—God would reveal the plan to Elisha, and Elisha would alert the troops. After several such instances, the king of Syria got word that Elisha was to blame. And that's when Elisha's servant got worried:

> So the king [of Syria] sent horses and chariots there with a strong army. They came at night and surrounded the city.
> Elisha's servant got up early and went out. He saw an army with horses and chariots surrounding the city. His servant said to Elisha, "Oh, no! Master, what will we do?"
> "Don't be afraid," Elisha said, "because there are more of us than there are of them." Then Elisha prayed, "LORD, please open his eyes that he may see." Then the LORD opened the servant's eyes, and he saw that the mountain was full of horses and fiery chariots surrounding Elisha. (2 Kings 6:14-17)

Elisha saw with the eyes of faith. Because he believed, he could see what his servant could not. When we focus on living a story of abundant faith, we begin to see things differently. Like the flip of a switch, suddenly faith illuminates a reality we never knew existed.

Before my family stepped out by faith to answer God's call in our own lives, we talked a lot about trusting God. All that talk suddenly became real when we committed to walking by faith, in spite of the many chances for failure that surrounded us. It took a while for us to see clearly that the One who was for us was greater than whatever might be against us. Just ask my wife, whose name happens to be *Faith*.

FAITH'S OWN PERSPECTIVE

When I told my wife that I had decided to answer God's call to put my strengths to work for the church at large, she responded enthusiastically, much like Pippin in *The Fellowship of the Ring*: "Great! Where are we going?" In spite of her enthusiastic support, our journey of faith has not been an easy one for a highly organized mother of six young children. As someone who thrives on predictability, she later confided that when asked about our life direction, it was extremely difficult for her to say, "I don't know." Reality hit hardest on the day we realized that all of our income—both hers and mine—was going to zero in just two weeks. Six hungry kids to feed, a mortgage to pay, plus all the usual bills—and God was not just our only backup plan, but our only plan. In the midst of that uncertainty, we sought and received clarity from God on relocating to Atlanta, nearly a thousand miles away from family and friends.

Suffice it to say that walking by faith left Faith feeling, on a good day, disheveled. Yet this is how my incredible wife describes having faith open her eyes:

> And at the beginning of our journey I was failing
> miserably. Even though I knew I shouldn't have
> been, I was thinking, *There is no way God is going
> to provide for us.* Maybe I was just being pessimis-
> tic. I knew God *could* provide for us, but I wasn't
> so sure he *would.* The truth is that I had never
> been forced to trust him, to see if he would be all I
> thought I believed him to be.

Since faith opened my eyes, I look more at possibilities now, at what *could* be. I can now see clearly that all things are possible for those who trust in him. I see more to life than what some call the American dream. I don't let the balance in the bank account control me anymore, because blessings aren't just money and possessions.

I see church differently. I used to see passionate people as weird. But now I think God must have really done a work in their lives for them to be full of such joy.

I see people differently because I know that they, too, could walk by faith. And I find it easier to identify someone who says he walks by faith when it's only on a surface level, because I recognize the same excuses I used to use—and sometimes still do.

I think that if we had been called to the mission field then, I would have said, "Are you nuts?!" But it's a lot easier to see possibilities now that my faith muscles have been stretched and exercised. Now if we were called to the mission field, I wouldn't think that was crazy at all!

Since faith opened our eyes, we are living the life of faith we never thought possible and seeing more possibilities for the future than we ever acknowledged. When you look at the story you are living now, what do you see?

CHECK YOUR COORDINATES

- Did Faith's perspective seem strange to you, or can you relate to her changed vision?

- How would you react if God asked you to step out without knowing where you were going?

- Would you describe your life as full of abundant possibilities or limited with few options?

WHAT FAITH CAUSES YOU TO SEE

When faith opens your eyes, you see things in ways you never did before. It's not that life changes—rather, you are awakened to a reality previously hidden from you. Here are just a few significant things you start viewing differently:

You See God as God

When most of us think about God, we tend to project ourselves onto him. We put God in a box that would fit us at our best. That doesn't inspire us with much hope, because we know our own limits pretty well. When we see him as he truly is, we see abundance personified. He isn't just really rich and well connected. He is *the* connection, the source of all riches. "In God we live, move, and exist" (Acts 17:28) and "without the Word [God] nothing came into being" (John 1:3). "The LORD can do whatever he wants in heaven or on earth" (Psalm 135:6), and "nothing is impossible for God" (Luke 1:37). He "is able to do

55

far beyond all that we could ask or imagine" (Ephesians 3:20), and "the LORD's eyes scan the whole world to strengthen those who are committed to him with all their hearts" (2 Chronicles 16:9). Faith causes you to see that if the infinite, eternal, unchangeable God is *for* you, how could it possibly matter who or what is *against* you?

In Scripture, when three friends faced a fiery furnace for refusing to bow to an idol, they spoke boldly because they knew no furnace was big enough to contain their God. Because they believed God could transform impossible to possible, they walked by faith—and revealed the majesty of God to a stunned royal audience (see Daniel 3).

You See People as Potential FaithWalkers

When our faith is focused on God, we believe in his power to work in other people the same faith he has worked in us. Remember the disciple often mislabeled *Doubting Thomas*, as if he should be forever identified by his struggle to believe? Sure, he balked at embracing what we would all call impossible, but who among us hasn't done that? The rest of the biblical accounts show Thomas as a guy who was all in. But in John 20, Thomas merely voiced the questions others were thinking but were afraid to ask. He wanted answers he could commit to and he refused to act as if he knew the answers when he didn't.

When faith opens our eyes, our hearts break for those around us who, like Thomas, struggle to believe, and our hearts rejoice when these people commit themselves to follow Christ wholeheartedly. According to historical sources, Thomas became the first missionary to India, where he died at the end of a spear as a true FaithWalker. When faith opens our eyes, we see people not for who they are now, but who they could be with rightly focused faith.

You See Challenges as Opportunities

When young David showed up to deliver food to his brothers and discovered a giant bad-mouthing the Almighty, he saw an opportunity to put his sniper-like slingshot skills to work for God's glory (1 Samuel 17). As Malcolm Gladwell explains in his book *David and Goliath*, it was David, not Goliath, who had a distinct advantage that day. Based on the biblical description, Goliath likely suffered from a physical condition known as acromegaly. In addition to the abnormal growth, he likely suffered from poor eyesight, which caused him to refer to David's single staff as many "sticks." The condition would also have meant he could only see well enough to fight in close, hand-to-hand combat. Consequently, a sharp-shooting lad with wicked slingshot ability had a tremendous tactical advantage.

But no one else saw that reality, because no one else saw with eyes opened by faith. Because David's faith was rightly focused on God, he saw the challenge as an opportunity. He acted on what he believed to be true and emerged as the victor.

You See Excuses for What They Are

Let's face it: we all use excuses to justify why we fail to walk by faith. Here are a few you may recognize:

"My budget's too tight. I can't afford to do that." This sounds like good stewardship, but it's often a lack of faith in our abundant God. When our family chose to answer the call to step

away from our safe, secure paycheck, we had no savings on which we could rely. Our hope had to be in God to provide for our needs. He did, though often in ways we never anticipated.

"I need to be practical. FaithWalking is too extreme." My wife explains, "My view was that walking by faith was not responsible. But I've learned that earthly definitions and God's definitions are two different things." Remember that in Christ's parable of the talents, the servants the king rewarded were those who took risks (Matthew 25:14-30).

"That calling is not for everyone." As I mentioned, when we began our journey, we heard many sincere friends say this, as if offering up a preemptive defense in case God asked them to step out by faith. Because it is true that God does not call everyone to do the same thing and in the same way, it sounds like a valid reason not to step out in faith. But imagine what would happen if a teacher asked a student for a homework assignment and the student smugly replied, "That homework assignment is not for everyone." The teacher would likely arch an eyebrow and ask, "Do you have *your* assignment or not?" You can't fool God by simply waving your hand and cooly proclaiming, "I am not the FaithWalker you seek."

"I just don't want to do it. It's inconvenient." Because many of us live in such prosperous settings, we tend to think that life should be uncomplicated and unfold according to our plans. But walking by faith is an adventure in which we are not in control. It can become uncomfortable and even dangerous, but it has great rewards. For those seeking safe, predictable lives, the appearance of brief comfort is their only reward.

"It doesn't sound fun." Walking by faith doesn't always fit

our entertainment-driven model of what an exciting life should be. We think *fun* means being catered to in a care-free, risk-free environment. But faith always involves risk, or it wouldn't be faith. Living a story worth telling is not about being chauffeured into heaven. Walking by faith may not be all kicks and giggles, but it is the truly adventurous life. As Mark Batterson reminds us, "If you're bored, one thing is for sure: You're not following in the footsteps of Christ."

You See Possible Where Most See Impossible

When Walt Disney began secretly buying up acres of land in central Florida, he could get it pretty cheap. As far as anyone else was concerned, buying swampland sounded like the punchline of a bad joke. And creating a massive theme park experience half the size of Manhattan in that area? Impossible.

But Walt saw differently because he believed differently. His belief sparked a vision for something no one else had ever attempted, not just theme parks but a futuristic city (Experimental Prototype Community of Tomorrow, EPCOT) that could serve as a proving ground for new technologies. Only after word escaped that Walt was the one buying up all the land did that swampland become some of the most expensive real estate in America.

More than fifty years after Walt purchased swampy acres, Walt Disney World remains the world standard for creating memorable experiences in a theme park setting. But it all began with one man seeing "the most magical place on Earth" where everyone else saw only swamp land. Everything is impossible— until somebody does it. To step away from a secure job and into the unknown with six kids and no backup plan? We thought it impossible until faith caused us to see things differently. Then, by God's grace, doing it didn't seem strange at all. Now as we reflect on what God has done in our story, we agree with Walt Disney: "It's kind of fun to do the impossible."

You See As If Instead of If Only

Peter and the rest of the disciples were being rocked on the Sea of Galilee by the storm to end all storms. The wind and waves tossed them around like a toy boat in a swimming pool full of excited children. You would think seeing Jesus walking on the water toward them would open their eyes, but only Peter saw an opportunity to walk by faith. No doubt the rest of the disciples responded as most of us would, rationalizing why walking to Jesus could never work: "*If only* the wind and waves would stop…" "*If only* I had a life jacket…" "*If only* I could walk on water…."

Peter saw things differently and began to shift from *if only* to *what if*. *What if I could trust Jesus so completely that I would get out of the boat and walk to him on the water?* His *what if* moved him to request permission to step overboard. Soon *what if* turned to *as if* as he felt the cool water on the soles of his feet. One foot followed the other as he walked *as if* all things were truly possible for God (Matthew 14:24-29). And here's something we often overlook: How did Peter get back to the boat after taking his eyes off Jesus and slipping beneath the waves? Matthew doesn't tell us Jesus carried the soaking-wet disciple or magically transported both of them back to the boat. Here is the most likely answer: Peter walked. On water. Again.

When faith opens our eyes, we see *if only* turn to *what if*, and *what if* transform into living *as if*. And that's where your story really gets good. But we can't even see ourselves living by faith, much less do it, unless faith opens our eyes.

 ## PREPARE YOUR GEAR

How to Check for Blind Spots in Your Faith

- **Acknowledge your perspective is not perfect.** No one has unobstructed vision, at least not on this side of eternity. Know that each person's faith is defective in some way that is often difficult to identify.

- **Engage in healthy self-examination.** Check yourself regularly by intentionally inspecting what you see from numerous perspectives. Measure what you see against what you believe to be true about God.

- **Beware of sudden disappearances.** When you are thinking about certain topics, do you find yourself shutting down or withdrawing from discussions with others? You may be avoiding issues you need to see more clearly.

- **Visit with a vision specialist.** Sometimes it takes a specialist to see what you can't. Enlist the help of a pastor or trusted advisor who shares your beliefs, has experience as a FaithWalker, and will speak the truth to you in love.

> • **Wear corrective lenses.** Borrow someone else's perspective on a regular basis to double-check your own take on life. Surround yourself with a community of FaithWalkers who will tell you the truth about what they see.

TO SEE OR NOT TO SEE

We tend to evaluate our life story by what we can see apart from faith, instead of by what we can see when faith opens our eyes. That's only natural. But when we consider reality from God's point of view, our perspective begins to change: "The things that can be seen don't last, but the things that can't be seen are eternal" (2 Corinthians 4:18).

According to this counterintuitive truth, if you can see something with your physical eyes, it is already in the process of fading away. Money in the bank account, houses in suburbia, granite memorials, works of art, corporate success, exquisite gardens, scrumptious food, charitable foundations, even Disney World: if you can see it, you're already losing it. This is not to say that we can't enjoy them all in the meantime, but living a life consumed by them will one day leave us with nothing.

Distinguishing between the temporary and the eternal, the seen and the unseen, wasn't always so difficult for us. When we were created, we understood the distinction between the two. God created us to tend a physical world of "the seen," yet we walked in close relationship with him who defines "the unseen." When in Eden we chose to focus our faith on ourselves instead of him, our ability to distinguish between the two vanished almost completely.

Because we were made in God's image, we didn't entirely lose our awareness of "the unseen," but "the seen" now dominated our perspective. But when Christ does his mightiest work of restoring us by faith to right relationship with him, he calls us "out of darkness into his amazing light" (1 Peter 2:9). We now can see, and not just as we did before, but better, as if through corrective lenses. Thanks to God's detailed revelation and the power of the Holy Spirit within us, we can see more than even Adam and Eve saw of "the unseen." "The seen" can still block our view, but only if we let it, for faith has opened our eyes.

Eventually, those of us whose hearts have been transformed by faith will rejoin our Maker, and our faith will become sight. In other words, one day there will no longer be any distinction between "the seen" and "the unseen" for "we'll see him as he is" (1 John 3:2). His reality will become our reality: "For now we see a reflection in a mirror; then we will see face-to-face" (1 Corinthians 13:12). And someday, for those whose faith is rightly focused, making that distinction will no longer be an issue.

Hebrews 11 is often called the Faith Hall of Fame because it praises those who lived stories of abundant faith:

> Through faith they conquered kingdoms, brought
> about justice, realized promises, shut the mouths of
> lions, put out raging fires, escaped from the edge of
> the sword, found strength in weakness, were mighty
> in war, and routed foreign armies. Women received

back their dead by resurrection. Others were tortured and refused to be released so they could gain a better resurrection.

But others experienced public shame by being taunted and whipped; they were even put in chains and in prison. They were stoned to death, they were cut in two, and they died by being murdered with swords. They went around wearing the skins of sheep and goats, needy, oppressed, and mistreated. The world didn't deserve them. They wandered around in deserts, mountains, caves, and holes in the ground. (Hebrews 11:33-38)

Clearly they lived stories worth telling, stories we are not even worthy to hear. They lived those stories because their gaze was not on "the seen" but on "the unseen." According to the writer of Hebrews, "All of these people died in faith without receiving the promises, but they saw the promises from a distance and welcomed them" (Hebrews 11:13). They understood that "the unseen" was permanent, and it gave them strength to suffer short-term discomfort to gain long-term significance. Because they saw what others would not see, they did what others could not do. As a result, their lives are the ones God himself highlights as if to say, "Now those are stories worth telling!"

When we refuse to walk by faith, we choose a story confined to "the seen," a fleeting tale already in the process of fading even as we live it. The best of us will leave little trace of our existence once our time has come and gone. But faith opens your eyes to the reality that we were not created just for the *present* but for the future. That truth is what must guide how we live our story, for that is where our story will prove to be worth telling. Right now, our story fades a little more each day in spite of our best efforts to ensure it cannot be forgotten. But when we live for what is coming—think of the Pereaus—our story can be one we never tire of telling, one that God himself will be proud to share.

If only we have the faith to see.

EXPLORE THE TRAIL AHEAD

- Take a moment now to recall times in your life when you have unmistakably seen God work. Perhaps when he supplied a need that seemed out of reach. Or restored an estranged friend after fervent prayer. Or gave healing for which there was no medical explanation. Maybe it was just a work of clarity in your own soul. List a few of those times now. Recall how your faith grew as a result and share with God in prayer how you would like to see it thrive once again.

- Describe a vision you've had or a dream that you think God may want you to pursue. It may seem as simple as developing a gift he has given or ministering to someone in need—or as complex as launching a new ministry, business, or outreach in your community. Take the time to write it down now. What first step can you take toward achieving it?

- Think about the excuses you are offering now for not fully pursuing the vision God has granted you or for not fully engaging life each day with greater faith. Which of your excuses do you think will hold up to God's scrutiny?

- There's an old adage that says, "Blessed is the man who aims at nothing, for he will surely hit it." At what are you aiming? Do you have a clear vision that drives you on your journey? If not, pause now to list some causes or dreams that fuel your passions.

FAITH THRIVES ON TRUTH

On a trip to speak in Guam, I spent a day on the island of Saipan with friends. Located just north of Guam and midway between Japan and New Guinea, Saipan once boasted a bustling garment industry. But when China began attracting clothing manufacturers near the end of the first decade of the new century, Saipan's economy shut down nearly overnight. Abandoned factories and shopping malls now litter the tropical paradise. The island had a strangely appropriate haunted feel, not just because of the emptied buildings, but because Saipan had been a battleground in World War II and the setting for a horrific instance of faith gone terribly wrong.

As I stood in the command bunker used by the Japanese during the war, I imagined what it must have been like to be Lieutenant General Yoshitsugu Saito on July 6, 1944. The desperate commander had retreated to this northern hideaway carved out of craggy rocks as United States Marines flooded the island. From that bunker, he gave the command for thousands of Japanese soldiers to make a *banzai* or suicide charge using whatever they could find as weapons. By the time the Marines repelled the attack, more than four thousand Japanese soldiers had died. Saito, shamed by his failure to hold the island, killed himself. His was only the first of many suicides that day.

To convince Japanese soldiers and civilians to valiantly resist the Americans, the Japanese government had spread propaganda about what American soldiers would do to all they captured. The Japanese people were told that if taken alive they would face rape, torture, and murder. From the top of Marpo Mountain along the northernmost tip of Saipan, I looked down on birds soaring far below me—and recoiled as I learned that hundreds of soldiers and civilians had leaped to their deaths from that very spot to avoid what they believed to be a worse fate if captured. With the surf crashing against the coral reefs eight hundred feet below, I would have thought it a place of exquisite beauty, were it not for the memory of nearly one thousand men, women, and children who jumped from the precipice. Marines recall watching helplessly as entire families stepped off the edge. Some parents even tossed their children first before following them to their watery graves. American soldiers used loudspeakers to communicate good intentions, but to no avail. Marines watched in horror as one group holding hand grenades leaped into the ocean from what would come to be known as Banzai Cliff. One by one, each held a grenade close—and pulled the pin.

Those unfortunate souls acted on what they believed to be true, but what they believed to be true was wrong. Their stories ended tragically because their source of truth was not truth at all, but propaganda.

THE PROPAGANDA WE FACE

Propaganda isn't only the stuff of war. Life and death also hang in the balance on this journey to live a story worth telling, so it's not surprising that we're bombarded with propaganda every day, presenting one of two extremes. Either it tells us to trust solely in what we see in this physical realm or it asks us to disconnect from truth entirely, take a blind leap, and call it *faith*. The reality is that we get fooled by this message more than we'd like to admit.

When we make decisions based solely on how much money is in the bank account, we believe the propaganda that money is scarce and must be hoarded. When we suppress that inner voice urging us to step out and do good in a radical way for fear of how it might affect our retirement plans, we're falling for the propaganda that this life is all there is. But the other extreme is to toss truth away entirely and just wing it. If the truth is that you have only five dollars in your bank account, you shouldn't pretend that isn't so. When someone chooses to "follow his heart" and walk away from a marriage because the romantic emotions he felt toward his spouse a decade ago are fading, he's falling for the propaganda that his shifting emotions are a reliable guide for living a story worth telling. Propaganda is so deceiving because it often contains a grain of truth, at least enough to be believable in the realm of the seen. But that's not all there is. Whenever we make decisions based solely on what we can see, sense, and feel, our story suffers for it. We need faith that thrives on truth to take righteous risks to live a story worth telling.

Choosing to step away from my role as a Christian school administrator took quite a bit of faith, but it wasn't of the "wing it" variety. On the one hand, we didn't have a robust savings account. (Few in ministry do.) But on the other hand, I knew that I had proven, marketable skills as a writer, communicator, and leader. I had education credentials and experience that could position me to provide for my family as God guided us forward. I didn't take the significant risk without realistically considering what I *could* see, sense, and feel.

But if I had evaluated *only* those criteria, I never would have stepped out. Although I had ideas of how the situation might work, few of them actually materialized. I could easily have stayed put from fear of the unknown, from fear of disappointing others, and from fear of what might happen if God didn't provide. Walking by faith means you step out before you know how it will all work out. But that doesn't mean your walk isn't grounded in truth.

The iconic film *Field of Dreams* (1989) tries to address both realms with the same advice. In the film, an impersonal voice tells the main character, a farmer, to plow under his corn, build a baseball field, and travel across the country for no apparent reason. The character chooses to "trust his heart" and follow the instructions, without any rational explanation. He puts his confidence in an unidentified, impersonal voice—and they all live happily ever after. It's a heartwarming film of faith, to be sure, but it's still a fairy tale. Faith rightly focused on God thrives when grounded in reality, because the source of all truth is, in fact, God himself.

CHECK YOUR COORDINATES

- Have you ever fallen for propaganda that has led your faith astray? When? What swayed you?

- Which extreme approach to faith do you tend to embrace: *trust what you can see* or *take a blind leap?*

- What righteous risks have you taken thus far in your story?

TRUTH IS A PERSON

When Thomas, the alleged doubting disciple, asked Jesus a gutsy question, Jesus answered with this stunning statement: "I am the way, the truth, and the life" (John 14:6). Many of the philosophers of that day viewed truth as something closer to the impersonal voice of *Field of Dreams*, or like a fate that governed loosely through logic and reason. When Jesus made this statement, he claimed to be truth personified. It was for this reason that John began his Gospel account with the radical claim that the Word (the *logos* from which we derive our word *logic*) was with God, the Word was God, and that the Word had made all things and continues to sustain them. He concluded his introduction by connecting that Word clearly to the person of Jesus: "The Word became flesh and made his home among us. We have seen his glory, glory like that of a father's only son, full of grace and truth" (John 1:14).

As God who had become man, Jesus said that he *is* the truth. That's why we can be confident that faith and truth are not enemies. The Source of all truth is also the One who works his mightiest work of faith within us. Like the two strands of polynucleotides that form DNA, faith and truth must weave together to fashion a story worth telling for all eternity. Thankfully, God has not left us guessing as to how to access this truth. We don't have to listen for voices in a cornfield or blindly believe whatever propaganda comes our way. Truth is a Person, become visible in Jesus, who is revealed for all time in the Word. As he prayed in the garden before his crucifixion, Jesus made this connection: "Make them holy in the truth; your word is truth" (John 17:17).

Jesus reinforced this connection between truth and the Word of God in many places. One of the clearest is recorded by John. Jesus described trusting in the truth of the Scriptures as foundational to trusting in him: "If you believed Moses, you would believe me, because Moses wrote about me. If you don't believe the writings of Moses, how will you believe my words?" (John 5:46-47). Jesus argued that believing in what Moses had written (the Scriptures) was necessary to fully trusting in him. If you won't believe what has been written by holy men inspired by the Holy Spirit, you will never trust in the One who inspired them. The truth communicated in his Word is inseparable from faith focused on God.

But more than that, our faith in God is activated and sustained by truth in his Word. We focus our faith on God only after we are exposed to and believe the truth it contains:

- Since childhood you have known the holy scriptures that help you to be wise in a way that leads to salvation through faith that is in Christ Jesus. (2 Timothy 3:15)

- We were the first to hope in Christ. You too heard the word of truth in Christ, which is the good news of your salvation. (Ephesians 1:12-13)

- Faith comes from listening, but it's listening by means of Christ's message. (Romans 10:17)

- We also had the good news preached to us, just as the Israelites did. However, the message they heard didn't help them because they weren't united in faith with the ones who listened to it. (Hebrews 4:2)

Faith and the truth of God's Word must go hand in hand from the start of our faith journey to its end. When God begins his work of faith within us, he does so by means of the truth in his Word. For that seed of faith to flourish, it must have access to that truth. Our faith cannot continue to grow or thrive unless it regularly feeds on his truth.

Trying to walk by faith without the Scriptures is like trying to eat a delicious bowl of creamy tomato soup with a fork. You may be able to get a taste of its goodness by licking the fork, but most of its benefit will elude you, and you'll make a mess in the process. In the same way, you will never know the supernatural power of a life lived with abundant faith—a story worth telling—unless your faith consistently feeds on truth from the One who is both the Source of all truth and the Author and Finisher of your faith.

How the Word Causes Faith to Thrive

The truth of the Scriptures is like a trail kit that contains the essentials every FaithWalker needs to thrive on the journey. We might envision it as a "living and powerful" backpack (Hebrews 4:12 NKJV) from which we pull all manner of tools to help us on this journey "from faith to faith" (Romans 1:17 NKJV). After all, "every scripture is inspired by God...so that the person who belongs to God can be equipped to do everything that is good" (2 Timothy 3:16-17).

Here are just some of the vital functions God's Word has in our journey:

- **Illumination.** As "a lamp before [our] feet and a light for [our] journey" (Psalm 119:105), the Bible is to us what Galadriel's phial was to the hobbits on their quest in *The Fellowship of the Ring*: "A light to you in dark places, when all other lights go out."

- **Instruction.** As the ultimate field guide, the Bible teaches us what we need to know about the trail ahead so we are not "destroyed from lack of knowledge" (Hosea 4:6).

- **Guidance.** Like a proven map, the Bible serves as the primary way God keeps his promise to "instruct you and teach you about the direction you should go" (Psalm 32:8).

- **Food.** Like a high-powered energy bar, the Bible gives you the nutrition you need so "your body will be healthy and your bones strengthened" for the journey (Proverbs 3:8).

- **Refreshment.** Like a bottle of cool water, the Word "reviv[es] one's very being," offering satisfaction that is "sweeter than honey—even dripping off the honeycomb" (Psalm 19:7, 10).

- **Orientation.** Like the North Star, the Word of God remains fixed forever in the heavens so we can always get our bearings, regardless of the conditions on the trail before us (Psalm 119:89).

- **Comfort.** Like a fire that gives warmth and security, the Bible assures us of God's promises and offers us rest even if the way is treacherous: "My comfort during my suffering is this: your word gives me new life" (Psalm 119:50).

- **Protection.** The Bible is "living, active, and sharper than any two-edged sword" (Hebrews 4:12), and it can defend you against threats that rise along the trail—*if* you have studied well to use it effectively.

- **Conviction.** Like a GPS receiver, it alerts you when you drift off course, advising you how best to recalculate, warning you when danger lies ahead (Psalm 19:11).

How to Engage the Word

I've tried all manner of methods to engage the Word in my nearly four-decade journey of faith. There isn't just one right way to do it. However, because I want to engage truth when I am at my most creative, I've found that mornings are my best time of day. Reading the Scriptures alongside my first cup of coffee brings my first thoughts of the day to God. Find your best, most engaged time of day. If you are a morning person, like me (and I've known very few Christians who read in an engaged way just prior to turning in for the night), try to jump-start your faith with truth at the beginning of every day. That time of day worked well for the psalmist: "I meet the predawn light and cry for help. I wait for your promise" (Psalm 119:147).

As to reading the Word, some Christians claim to be engaging the Bible by opening pages at random and blindly choosing a verse. But imagine if you tried that approach while hiking a trail. What if at every fork in the path you reached into your supply kit and used whatever you happened to pull out? Not surprisingly, you'd end up disillusioned if you expected matches to give direction, or a map to keep you warm. Similarly, different parts of God's Word apply to different decisions in your life. To know what passage or principle might apply, you have to spend time systematically or purposefully studying it. When life's inevitable challenges test your faith, you can better trust in the truth you need for your situation. The more you study it, the more familiar you become with what is in it. Engaging the Word is a process that continuously feeds your faith, causing it to grow over time—not in an instant.

Making sense of Scripture is often as much an art as a science. Two of the best resources I have found for understanding the Bible are *How to Read the Bible for All It's Worth* by Gordon D. Fee and Douglas Stuart and *Knowing Scripture* by R. C. Sproul. These are reliable sources to help you make sense of the big picture of basic Bible study.

But there is no shortage of different (and helpful) study methods:

- **Study a particular book of the Bible.** You can select a book, delve deeply into the story behind it, and even read through it several times. The Epistles (New Testament) and Prophets (Old Testament) are especially good for this approach.

- **Use a devotional guide.** You can always benefit from other FaithWalkers gifted in unpacking and applying truth in Scripture. Devotional guides offer a biblical passage and accompanying thoughts or a relevant story to motivate your own meditations.

- **Partner with fellow FaithWalkers.** You can invite a veteran trail guide to join you by reading a book he or she has written on a particular topic. I've enjoyed many such guides, including A. W. Tozer (*The Pursuit of God*), Tim Keller (*Counterfeit Gods*), and James Montgomery Boice (*Christ's Call to Discipleship*), to name just a few. Many voices are out there. Just be sure to study Scripture for yourself to see if what you read lines up with the truth. You may want to invite other FaithWalker friends to join you for a study. After all, Scripture reminds us that "Two are better than one because they have a good return for their hard work" (Ecclesiastes 4:9).

- **Read through the Bible chronologically.** You can read Scripture in the order in which it was written. This approach lets you see God's gradual revealing of himself to his creation. It can take a while, but the process of soaking in the Word in the order God gave it to us is worth it. Although many study editions of the Bible have chronological guides, a good tool to guide in this process is *The Chronological Guide to the Bible: Explore God's Word in Historical Order* (2010) that works with any translation.

- **Follow a topical study.** When you know you need help in a particular area, studying passages on that topic can be quite helpful. *Faith, temptation, anxiety, priorities*: all are frequently visited topics. Many Bibles have a topical index in the back. If yours doesn't, a quick Internet search can work just as well.

HOW TO READ THE BIBLE EVERY DAY— AND ENJOY IT

You may be thinking, *I know I should read the Bible, but it just doesn't sound appealing.* Perhaps it feels like a mysterious process for which you've never been given the secret decoder ring. Over the years, I've distilled a few tips into an acronym that's easy to remember and use each day. If you've a system that works better, by all means, stick with it. But if you could use a simple format to start reading the Bible every day, try to PRAY.

Pray

After you have found a quiet place, begin with prayer. You may need a few quiet minutes of reflection to shift the focus from busy, self-centered thoughts to God's thoughts. Some think about the vastness of God's power in nature and the reality of his holiness before confessing their failures as they come to mind. Confession quickly moves our reflections to the cross, where we remember the redeeming sacrifice of Christ. Finish by recalling Jesus' glorious resurrection and the coming eternal reality ahead.

I begin with prayer because I have no hope of truly understanding this divine revelation of "the unseen" unless the Giver of all wisdom reveals it to me. And so I pray, "Open my eyes so I can examine the wonders of your Instruction!" (Psalm 119:18). Apart from the Author's supernatural illumination, there's simply no way I *could* enjoy the Word, for "the Spirit is the one who testifies, because the Spirit is the truth" (1 John 5:6). So it is the Spirit, not my own cleverness, who causes me to see and delight in the truth I desperately need for life direction.

Read

This point would seem rather obvious, except that according to the latest surveys more than seven hundred people stop reading the Bible every day. Although Scripture is curiously silent about the casual reading of the Bible, it says a lot about intentional reading and careful study. Once I've chosen a plan for reading, I always have a notepad, an app, or some handy method to jot down questions, comments, or topics for further study. As a father of six children, I don't always have time to unpack the truth of Scripture as I read. But I want to keep my thoughts organized for easy follow-up. I try to schedule time each week, perhaps on a Saturday morning or Sunday afternoon, to circle back and get answers. With the many Bible study tools available via the Internet, it's never been easier to dig deep, to get answers that empower your faith to thrive on truth in Scripture.

Analyze

After reading a passage, pause and think about it. I find it helpful to identify the key verse or phrase that resonated with me most. I'll jot it on a Post-it, write it on my calendar, or put it somewhere I will be sure to see it again throughout the day. In this way, I remind myself to meditate all day, letting the truth soak into my life. The psalmist tells us that when we meditate on Scripture, really turn it over in our minds, we experience abundant growth, find lasting fulfillment, and gain the strength to weather life's storms (Psalm 1).

You

I know "you" doesn't fit with the list of verbs in the acronym, but that's kind of the point. I am not a verb. I am a person. The Word of God was given to transform my heart. So I finish each session by asking how the truth uncovered affects my life. Where has it revealed a lack of faith? What encouragement has it brought to my soul? What change is required in my attitude, behavior, or relationships? In short, how might my story be better because I engaged the truth today?

Scripture warns us not to deceive ourselves: when you encounter the Word of truth but don't apply it to your story, it's as if you've looked at your face in a mirror and then walked away, completely forgetting what you saw (James 1:22-25). What's the point of that? If you reach the end of your time engaging Scripture and still don't have anything to show for it, note that the pray acronym itself points to the solution. Return to the first step and pray for more of the wisdom God has promised all who ask in faith (James 1:5). In that sense, it's kind of like shampoo: instead of "lather, rinse, repeat," try "pray, read, repeat as needed." Once we have direction from this most reliable guide, we can experience God's blessings each and every day, and we can know his joy as we make choices that align with the wisdom we've discovered.

 ## Prepare Your Gear

In Case of Emergency, Break Out Three Proven Plans

It's easy to drift away from truth and into propaganda between Bible reading plans. Here are three proven plans to guide you when you don't know what to read next:

- **Read the Proverbs.** Solomon's book of wisdom makes for the ideal default plan: its thirty-one chapters automatically correlate with the days of the month and each verse is already broken down into bite-size morsels.

- **Read the Psalms.** Another book easily divisible by thirty, reading five chapters a day will get you through the book of Psalms in a month and expose you to a variety of moods, prayers, and praises. If that pace feels too aggressive, just take a chapter a day.

- **Read the life of Christ.** Learn more about Jesus. The four accounts of the life of Christ (Matthew, Mark, Luke, and John) read a lot like stories—because they are true stories. And because each writer focuses on different themes, you'll discover an often-missed depth to Christ's story by reading them together.

IN CASE OF EMERGENCY, INJECT TRUTH

If you suffer from severe allergic reactions or know some-one who does, you know how critical an epinephrine injection can be in case of emergency. When someone with an allergy to bee stings is stung, for example, she has only moments to inject the medication to counteract the life-threatening effects. So it is with faith and truth. When propaganda first begins to disrupt our faith, we may have only moments to inject a healthy dose of truth before the damage begins.

Jesus himself kept truth at the ready for just such a crisis of faith. After three years of ministry, he found himself surround-ed by disciples who seemed clueless about his intentions. Even worse, they tried to conceal the fact that they had no clue. Jesus had just been explaining his future death and ascension and the coming of the Holy Spirit. In John 16 the disciples said among themselves, "What does he mean: 'Soon you won't see me, and soon after that you will see me' and 'Because I'm going to the Father'? What does he mean by 'soon'? We don't understand what he's talking about" (vv. 17-18).

After Jesus tried explaining yet again, they responded much the way you and I might have:

"His disciples said, 'See! Now you speak plainly; you aren't using figures of speech. Now we know that you know everything and you don't need anyone to ask you. Because of this we believe you have come from God'" (vv. 29-30).

In what has to be the worst case of pandering ever recorded in Scripture, the disciples basically said, "We have no idea what you are talking about, but we'll say something that we think you'll like hearing." Jesus' next response was understandably direct: "Now you believe?" (v. 31). After three years, *now* you claim to understand the most basic truth I've taught you? You're just saying that so you don't look stupid!

At that precise moment, I believe Jesus faced a temptation to which you and I can easily relate. Everything he could see, sense, and feel said his mission was a failure. I imagine he was tempted to think something like this: *My own disciples don't get it. No one gets it. I don't see any results—and I'm almost out of time.* You can hear the war within when he responded, "Look! A time is coming—and is here!—when each of you will be scattered to your own homes and you will leave me alone." But it's what Jesus said next that shows us how to react when our own faith wavers in a crisis: "I'm not really alone, for the Father is with me" (v. 32).

Jesus injected truth when facing the temptation to waver. He plunged a syringe full of reality into his thinking. The truth was that he was not alone, no matter what he might see, sense, or feel. The Father was with him always. Jesus' grasp on truth meant he could face any challenge, endure any discouragement, and continue to thrive on his journey.

The time to prepare for a crisis of faith is long before your faith is in crisis. A crisis—including falling for propaganda—does not cause your faith to crumble; it simply reveals the strength of your faith. By maintaining a steady diet of truth, and being ready for an emergency injection, your faith will be equipped to respond to any circumstances. And you will be prepared to live a story that is truly worth telling.

EXPLORE THE TRAIL AHEAD

- Have you ever been tempted like Jesus to think you are all alone or that your situation is hopeless? Is your truth injection ready? Take a moment now to jot down specific temptations with which you struggle. Then add biblical truths that can give you hope during those seasons of disorientation.

- First Corinthians 1:27 tells us that "God chose what the world considers foolish" to be a critical catalyst for our faith growth. Are you part of a church community that feeds your faith through preaching aligned with God's Word? If not, it may be time to find another church where your faith can thrive on a steady diet of truth each week. If so, are you taking full advantage of it by prayerfully preparing yourself, taking careful notes for later study, and applying what you hear to your daily walk?

- The Bible can be both incredibly simple and quite sophisticated. Check with your church this week to see what classes may be available to learn more about this critical tool.

- Commit to reading the Bible each morning for the next twenty-one days. Schedule fifteen to twenty minutes of alone time. Ask God to open the eyes of your heart so you can see and know him. Then follow the PRAY acrostic to engage his Word.

- Make an effort to remember the main point of what you read when you encounter God's Word. Expect to find something valuable each time and plan to record it in some way that will keep it before you throughout the day. It may be as simple as a sticky note or as high-tech as a note-taking app.

6

Faith Finds a Voice

I've mentioned that in April 2012, my wife and I decided that God was calling me to step away from my position at Cornerstone Christian Academy after helping to launch and lead it for a dozen years. As we anticipated our income's drop to zero, we sought counsel on our next steps. I could not shake the sense that, in spite of having no money, we were supposed to leave northeast Ohio, where my wife and I had lived our entire lives, and move nearly a thousand miles away to Atlanta, Georgia.

It was just a feeling at first, but then it began to make sense for a number of reasons. I had begun connecting with a lot of like-minded people in Atlanta. I wanted to put my gifts to work as a catalyst for God's work, and as the "buckle of the Bible belt," Atlanta is a hotspot for Christian organizations. It's also a key travel hub and gets less snow in a year than Ohio gets in one day. We'd even found a church that would be a good fit. After wrestling with this choice for some weeks, a few key friends advised me to pray diligently for wisdom and then make a decision.

I did as they suggested and received the clarity I requested. We would move to Atlanta to better position ourselves to answer God's call to equip Christians to think, live, and lead with abundant faith. Because we believed God had called us to move, we started doing what needed to be done, in spite of what we saw, sensed, or felt. Once I'd left my job, we had no money to pay our mortgage anyway, so the sooner the house sold, the better. By early October, our house went on the market. But nobody came.

We prayed bold prayers, fully expecting God to make a way for us to follow his lead by faith. We had already seen God provide for our needs in unexpected ways, which had grown our faith. So I began praying a very specific prayer. I was scheduled to journey to the other side of the world to speak at an Equip Leadership conference in Guam in early November. And so I prayed expectantly and vigorously that God would have our house under contract by the time my flight left the ground. When that did not happen, I was disillusioned, struggling for confidence.

On the twenty-four-hour flight to Guam, I was wrestling with God, trying to figure out why he had not answered my focused, intentional prayer to sell our house quickly. Just before my trip, my life coach had given me a copy of a book by Mark Batterson, *The Circle Maker: Praying Circles Around Your Biggest Dreams and Greatest Fears*. As I flew, I read, "Sometimes what we perceive as a period is really just a comma. We think that God's silence is the end of the sentence, but it's just a providential pause."

As I read Mark's words at thirty thousand feet, somewhere

over the Pacific Ocean, a light came on. I don't know if I accidentally pushed the flight attendant call button or if the rarefied air caused me to inhale a divine thought, but God's message couldn't have been clearer:

God: "Do you believe that I have called you to go to Atlanta?"

Me: "Yes."

God: "Do you believe that I will answer your prayer and provide for your needs as I promised?"

Me: "Um, yes."

God: "Then what's the problem? You prayed. I answered."

Me: "Well, yes, but—"

God: "Your house is already sold. I just haven't told you the details yet."

AND THE WALLS CAME TUMBLING DOWN

From this emboldened perspective, my faith found a new voice—one of confidently praising God for the work God had already done, even though we didn't know how or to whom. When I returned home in mid-November, I described the approach to my wife and our six children. Then I proposed something kind of weird: to help us focus our faith and put our praise into action, we'd actually walk around the house, circling it as each one of us prayed. We'd thank God for selling our house and ask him to reveal the details in his time and in his way.

Incredibly, they all agreed to the plan. It was November in northeast Ohio, after all, which meant snow, cold, and generally uncomfortable conditions. But we did it. We decided to follow the example set by the Israelites when they walked around the walls of Jericho and waited for God to cause the walls to come tumbling down (see Joshua 6). We walked around the house once a day for six days, each time praying and thanking God for answering our prayer. I will never forget hearing our children boldly claiming God's promises in prayer while trusting him to handle the specifics when he was ready.

On the seventh day, we walked around seven times and sang songs of praise. I half-expected the walls of the house to fall, but nothing happened. We kept praying inside the house as well. And I took that same walk many more times myself, immersed in the same silent prayer as we waited. And waited. And waited. For five more months we waited. No income. No clear direction. Nothing but silence.

It was during those months of seemingly endless and unproductive house-showings that I began to feel what the poet Robert Frost described as being "far in the sameness of the woods." Every day started to look the same. All too often I gave in to the temptation of wondering if God had, in fact, forgotten our prayer. As I poured out my heart to God, my prayers frequently ended with an emphatic *Why?*

By the time we reached April 2013—a year after we initially answered God's call to step out by faith—I was almost ready to quit. Based on what we could see, our financial situation was about as bleak as it could be. Our house had been on the market for six months and was no closer to being sold. We hadn't received any offers that would allow us to walk away from it without paying someone to take it off our hands, let alone have any money left with which to move to Atlanta. So we reluctantly told our real estate agent to take it off the market. We left the children with generous grandparents while my wife and I regrouped on one of my regular ministry trips to Guam. We still believed—most days—that God had answered our prayers but just hadn't filled in the blanks yet.

It was only after we returned from Guam that God shared with us the highlights of his plan. Only then did some family members stop over unexpectedly to chat and reveal to us that they thought—wait for it—that God wanted *them* to buy our house. By that time, I was too numb to process it. I might have mumbled a groggy, "What?" As we talked it through, we discovered the move would make sense for them for a number of very practical reasons. As we began to talk actual numbers, the beauty of God's plan became clear. The house hadn't sold previously in part because agents' fees made it difficult to find a price at which a buyer could get a good deal and we could have money left over to move. Now, after waiting for six months, the way was finally clear to sell the house for less and yet walk away with more.

So the house was sold. I'm not suggesting this as a new way to sell real estate. But our story demonstrates that, in order to live a story worth telling, your faith must first find its voice through confident prayer—even if it takes a while to fully understand. We also learned to treasure God's mercy as we wrestled through a season of doubt and uncertainty. Chuck DeGroat describes that counterintuitive blessing in this way: "Struggle opens up the possibility of an invasion of God's grace, a moment of rescue and redemption." What challenges are you facing now in your own story and how might God be using it to help you find your voice?

CHECK YOUR COORDINATES

- When was the last time you stepped out by faith without knowing all the details?

- Do you struggle to admit frustration when God doesn't seem to hear your voice?

- Do you think of adversity as an opportunity for God's grace or a sign of his rejection?

THE SONG FAITH SINGS

Faith with no voice, or faith that is not expressed, probably isn't faith at all. The psalmist put it bluntly: "I believed, therefore I spoke" (Psalm 116:10 NKJV). If what you believe to be true doesn't lead you to authentically express that faith in some way, do you really believe it? In our situation, our faith expressed itself first through prayer, both by pleading with God to provide and by praising him for the answer he was in the process of giving. In fact, if faith is *doing what you believe to be true,* then prayer is often the very first thing we do. Richard Cecil expresses it this way: "Prayer is faith passing into action." Like the symbiotic relationship between faith and truth, faith moves us to pray, and prayer moves us to greater faith.

The Apostle Paul, who called us to walk by faith and not by sight, solidifies the connection between finding our faith and discovering its voice: "Since we have the same spirit of faith, according to what has been written, 'I believed and therefore I spoke,' we also believe and therefore speak" (2 Corinthians 4:13 NKJV). Jesus himself reinforced this connection between what we believe and what we vocalize: "What fills the heart comes out of the mouth" (Matthew 12:34). Your voice expresses what you believe to be true. What you believe cannot help but come out.

Faith can find a voice in a variety of ways: singing, journaling, sharing our story, teaching, proclaiming, and more. But prayer is the primary means through which faith speaks. Put another way, prayer is the core melody at the heart of our song of faith. It is the basic tune we whistle while strolling the trail of day-to-day life. It is the simple refrain every FaithWalker struggles to hum while groping through life's darkest nights. Although other voices may join in our broader symphony of faith, prayer sets the tone for them all to ensure the fullest, most robust expression. Without prayer to guide them, our expressions of faith will sound more like a chaotic orchestra tune-up than a unified celebration that reveals the majesty of God.

If we don't believe, we won't pray. If we don't pray, can we truly be living a story of faith, a story worth telling?

FAITH'S PRIMARY VOICE

J. C. Ryle said, "Faith is to the soul what life is to the body. Prayer is to faith what breath is to the body. How a person can live and not breathe is past my comprehension, and how a person can believe and not pray is past my comprehension too."

Jude wrote, "But you, dear friends: build each other up on the foundation of your most holy faith, pray in the Holy Spirit, keep each other in the love of God" (20-21).

FaithWalkers from Jude to Ryle's time agree: we keep ourselves on the right path by building our faith *and* praying. The two are inextricably intertwined. E. M. Bounds, one of the most influential voices on prayer in the last two centuries, uses another picture: "Prayer and faith are like Siamese twins. One heart animated them both. Faith is always praying. Prayer is always believing."

We often succumb to a self-defeating cycle of disbelief that stifles our faith before it ever finds a voice. Because we don't *see* the mighty works of God, we don't believe. Because we don't *believe*, we don't *pray*. Because we fail to *pray*, we don't *see* the mighty works of God. And so it goes. (Remember that living by faith means acting on what we believe to be true, often in spite of what we see.) This downward spiral of disbelief is shattered only when we choose first to believe and then to pray with confidence. Mark Batterson reminds, "The greatest tragedy in life is the prayers that go unanswered because they go unasked." James himself said, "You don't have because you don't ask" (James 4:2). But we must first believe God's promises to be true *before* we will ever ask to receive. Only then will we see God work in ways that embolden us to ask for more, and a much better cycle will begin.

Prayer can get a bad rap as an excuse for inactivity, as if only people who can't make their own choices pause to pray. Our action-oriented culture tends to view prayer as doing nothing, but Oswald Chambers describes it differently:

We tend to use prayer as a last resort, but God
wants it to be our first line of defense. We pray
when there's nothing else we can do, but God wants
us to pray before we do anything at all....Most of
us would prefer, however, to spend our time doing
something that will get immediate results. We don't
want to wait for God to resolve matters in His good
time because His idea of "good time" is seldom in
sync with ours.

Prayer is not just a good back-up option; it is the most powerful thing you can do. It puts supernatural forces into motion that
are beyond our comprehension. As E. M. Bounds poignantly
said, "Prayer is but the request of man for God, through the
Holy Spirit, to interfere on behalf of him who prays." Asking the
Almighty *to interfere on our behalf* takes courage, a boldness
that can flow only from God's having first done his mightiest
work of faith within us. That's not to say that we should pray
and then do nothing. But as Dr. A. J. Gordon wisely noted, "You
can do more than pray *after* you have prayed, but you cannot
do more than pray *until* you have prayed."

Prayer itself is an act of

- **Surrender.** There's a reason we talk about bowing in
  prayer. When we pray, we acknowledge God's authority over us: "Our Father who is in heaven, uphold the
  holiness of your name" (Matthew 6:9).

- **Humility.** When we pray, we acknowledge that we
  don't know it all; we need God's help. God exalts

those who humble themselves before him (James 4:10).

- **Relationship.** Words establish relationships, with God and with one another. When we converse with God in prayer, we engage in the challenging but rewarding work of relationship-building. "I'm standing at the door and knocking. If any hear my voice and open the door, I will come in to be with them, and will have dinner with them, and they will have dinner with me" (Revelation 3:20).

- **Passion.** The psalmist tells us, "Pour out your hearts before him! God is our refuge!" (Psalm 62:8). The word translated "pour" literally means "to empty it all out." Real prayer can be pretty messy. But God welcomes the trusting soul who authentically lays it all before his throne.

- **Persistence.** Jesus warned that we often fail to get what we ask for because we knock once and give up (see Luke 11:5-10). Instead, prayer should be marked by dogged persistence that exercises our faith as it moves God to "interfere" for us.

- **Praise.** The first thing Jesus instructs us to do in prayer is to "hallow" or exalt the name of God (Matthew 6:9 NKJV). "I give thanks to you with all my heart, LORD. I sing your praise before all other gods" (Psalm 138:1): a heart full of praise in prayer will lead others to praise.

- **Worship.** "God is spirit, and it is necessary to worship God in spirit and truth" (John 4:24). We are to offer him worship when unseen by others. Personal prayer filled with worship paves the way for worship that is lived out before others.

- **Preparation.** When Job cried out to God in the midst of adversity, he discovered that he was not yet ready to receive God's answer (Job 40:3-5; 42:1-6). The very act of prayer itself can prepare us for what's next. Tim Elmore, author of *Pivotal Praying*, notes, "It is more important that I be changed in prayer than that prayer change my circumstances."

- **Patience.** One of the greatest challenges to our faith occurs when we appear to receive no answer from God at all. Those occasions try our faith, but James tells us, "The testing of your faith produces endurance. Let this endurance complete its work so that you may be fully mature, complete, and lacking in nothing" (James 1:3-4).

STIRRING UP YOUR FAITH

Inactivity in our prayer life leads inevitably to paralysis in our faith walk. Not praying leads quickly to not doing. On this journey to live a story worth telling, you'll encounter Christians who used to pray with passion and live with abundant faith. But now they've settled in and gotten comfortable somewhere along the way. Instead of leaning in to the challenges of the trail to the summit, they've set up a souvenir shop where tired Christians can relax, slap a sticker on their backpack, and pick up a T-shirt—or even start a treadmill franchise of their own. The truth is that left to ourselves, we tend to settle for the easy option. Of that tendency, D. L. Moody noted, "He who kneels the most, stands the best." Our faith must be stirred frequently by fervent prayer lest we drift into living a story no one wants to hear.

Just ask the disciples who followed Jesus during his time on earth. Because they had experienced some success, they became comfortable. When a man brought his demon-possessed son to them for help, they tried to cast it out—and failed miserably. The worst part was that all of their critics were watching. By the time Jesus arrived on the scene, the disciples were actually arguing with their critics and creating quite a commotion. Talk about an embarrassing scene! Check out how Jesus responded to the chaos:

> Jesus asked them, "What are you arguing about?"
> Someone from the crowd responded, "Teacher, I brought my son to you, since he has a spirit that doesn't allow him to speak. Wherever it overpowers him, it throws him into a fit. He foams at the mouth, grinds his teeth, and stiffens up. So I spoke to your disciples to see if they could throw it out, but they couldn't."
> Jesus answered them, "You faithless generation, how long will I be with you? How long will I put up with you? Bring him to me."

They brought him. When the spirit saw Jesus, it immediately threw the boy into a fit. He fell on the ground and rolled around, foaming at the mouth. Jesus asked his father, "How long has this been going on?"

He said, "Since he was a child. It has often thrown him into a fire or into water trying to kill him. If you can do anything, help us! Show us compassion!"

Jesus said to him, "'If you can do anything'? All things are possible for the one who has faith."

At that the boy's father cried out, "I have faith; help my lack of faith!"

Noticing that the crowd had surged together, Jesus spoke harshly to the unclean spirit, "Mute and deaf spirit, I command you to come out of him and never enter him again."

After screaming and shaking the boy horribly, the spirit came out. The boy seemed to be dead; in fact, several people said that he had died.

But Jesus took his hand, lifted him up, and he arose.

After Jesus went into a house, his disciples asked him privately, "Why couldn't we throw this spirit out?"

Jesus answered, "Throwing this kind of spirit out requires prayer." (Mark 9:16-29)

Stories of faith failures like this always give me hope because I know most of the disciples' stories turned out to be ones worth telling. In this instance, however, they were too embarrassed even to answer Jesus when he asked what was happening. Yet Jesus cut right to the heart of the problem: their faith lacked power to perform because they lacked a focus on prayer. The disciples forgot that the source of their faith was also the source of their strength. They had started setting up a souvenir shop to rest on previous successes, when what their faith truly needed was continual stirring to cry out for more. They failed to realize that faith is always in motion, but prayer keeps it moving in the right direction.

Your quest to live a story worth telling is no different. When prayer has faded from your schedule, your faith is not far behind. Our lack of prayer is evidence that we have begun to focus our faith somewhere other than on the Almighty. When your faith fails to express itself, it's not because it is resting but because it is dying. Your faith may feel like it's going fuzzy around the edges because it lacks the clarity that comes from regularly pouring out your heart to God.

WHEN WE FAIL TO PRAY

We easily become proud of such little success. When the Israelites barely managed to survive the journey from Egypt to Canaan, they got cocky and refused to enter the Promised Land by faith (see Numbers 13–14). They settled for the familiar confines of the wilderness until all but two of the adults who'd left Egypt had died—and their stories ended. Like the disciples, they thought they knew the situation. They thought they had everything under control. They were stunned back into reality when circumstances revealed their faith was no longer fully focused on God. By the time they realized their mistake, it was too late.

Likewise, if you have stopped praying, it may be that you've started thinking you know the trail well enough to get by on your own. The problem is, you've never walked this path before. As the investment advertisements remind us, past performance is not indicative of future results.

Lack of prayer makes us vulnerable to attack, and the enemy knows it, even if you don't. When you begin to think, *I've got this one*, you can be sure you have no clue what you're doing. T. D. Jakes puts it bluntly: "Whenever you face all of your problems and you trust only your plans to get you out—it is a sign that your faith is deteriorating." And when you realize that your faith has lost its voice, know that you are about to collapse without an immediate truth injection.

I served in retail management for a well-known chain for a few years back in the late 1990s. One night, I saw this tension between crying out for help and settling for comfort play out in real life. Back in those younger years, I led the team responsible for merchandise flow, essentially moving stuff from the trucks to the shelves for shoppers. We were headed into the busy Christmas season and had begun to work overnight while the store was closed. One young woman on my team (I'll call her July) was a diligent worker—one of the best—and a diabetic. She always kept food nearby as she worked, just in case her blood sugar levels dipped unexpectedly.

One night as I made my rounds, I discovered July missing. Her work cart was there, her purse and even her snacks were still there, but she was gone. After checking all the usual spots,

I raised the alarm and recruited others to help me search, but to no avail. It was as if she had vanished from a locked building without a trace. Finally, I had a crazy thought of one place we hadn't checked: the dressing rooms. There she was, huddled in the corner of the changing booth in the farthest corner of the store. By then she was nonresponsive, her lips discolored.

We immediately called the paramedics who, fortunately, were just across the street from the store. As they wheeled her out, they told us that she had nearly slipped into a diabetic coma. If we hadn't found her when we did, she probably would have died. As I reflected on the close call for July, I realized that in her disoriented state, she had chosen a cozy corner in the dressing room instead of crying out for help—and nearly died because of it.

On this journey to live a story worth telling, we tend to respond to life the way July did to her plunging blood-sugar levels. We stop moving when and where we feel comfortable. But comfort should never be confused with safety. The disciples rocking in the boat with Jesus during a raging storm were incredibly uncomfortable yet infinitely safe (Luke 8:22-25). Francis Chan is often quoted as saying, "God doesn't call us to be comfortable. He calls us to trust Him so completely that we are unafraid to put ourselves in situations where we will be in trouble if He doesn't come through." It is the height of irony that the very thing we fear—relying wholly and completely on God—is the only thing that can give what we crave: safety and security. As some pastor once said, "The second most dangerous place you can be is in the will of God." The first is wandering on your own.

PREPARE YOUR GEAR

How Fasting Empowers Your Faith

The spiritual practice of fasting is not a popular one in our desire-driven culture that markets instant gratification as the key to happiness—but it is an effective means for strengthening faith. Fasting is simply going without something good (usually food) for a season in order to focus more fully on something else, usually God. Here are a few benefits for FaithWalkers who engage in this timeless discipline:

- **Fasting sharpens your ability to see the unseen.** Jesus said, "As long as I am with you, you don't need to fast. But when I am gone, that's another story" (see Matthew 9:15). Fasting enables you to see more clearly what is not physically before you.

- **Fasting focuses your faith.** Like a malfunctioning digital camera that keeps zooming crazily in and out, our faith often loses focus. Eventually, our faith will become self-focusing, but fasting helps return it to its factory settings.

- **Fasting conditions us to trust.** Many Christians' faith muscles have atrophied because we don't seem to need them very much. When you make fasting part of your regular faith-building regimen, you condition yourself to be godly, as Paul advises in 1 Timothy 4:7.

- **Fasting trains us to live by faith.** Fasting forces our faith to be strengthened before it is tested. When we make a habit of depending on God in the little things, we find it easier to trust him throughout our story.

- **Fasting accelerates our growth.** When united with prayer, fasting acts as a catalyst for faith transformation. It strips us of our reliance on ourselves faster than would otherwise be possible.

Note: Always consult a physician before undertaking a fast.

MAKING TIME TO PRAY

The truth is that prayer changes everything, especially you. Yet many FaithWalkers take an accidental approach to prayer rather than carve out time and space for intentional communion with God. They pray as they go through life, sort of like grabbing whatever food is handy throughout the day. That practice may quench the hunger pangs at the moment, but it doesn't make for a healthy diet. I call it "multitasking prayer," and it can have disastrous results. Like texting and driving, it is deceptively dangerous because we appear to get away with it many times before disaster actually strikes. Much research has now demonstrated that texting and driving can slow the reaction time of a driver to the same extent as if he or she were drunk. I can't help but think that God must hear our hurried, distracted prayers at times and wonder whether we are more than slightly inebriated.

The common defense for multitasking prayer is this: Scripture tells us to pray without ceasing (1 Thessalonians 5:17), keeping an attitude of nonstop prayer, as stuff comes to mind throughout the day. Yet many use this to turn from intentional continual prayer to a set of accidental prayers, which don't form a full communion with God. When that happens, we quickly become like the hiker who snacks on energy bars all day instead of pausing by the trail to prepare balanced, nutritious meals. The quick bites of fellowship with the Almighty may satisfy some immediate hunger pang, but if that's the complete diet, your faith will soon become lean and malnourished, unfit to respond when tested.

Imagine how your life would be different if you spent three hours every day in focused, intentional prayer. Most of us believe we wouldn't get much else done. And yet here is the counterintuitive way one man described his take on focused, intentional prayer: "I have so much to do today that I will spend the first three hours in prayer." The man's name was Martin Luther. As a key figure of the Reformation, he lived a story of tremendous worth. His thinking leads us to this conclusion: if you think you don't have time to pray, that's exactly when you know you should.

Another person who accomplished great things for God, most notably helping to bring an end to the horrific slave trade of his day, was William Wilberforce. Though he seemed to be always in motion, this dynamo for justice recognized that he was too weak to do worthy work when he failed to make time to pray: "The shortening of private devotions starves the soul; it grows lean and faint. I have been keeping too late hours." Most revealing of all, Jesus himself regularly took time to step away from the crowds and hurried pace in order to pray (Mark 1:35; Luke 11:1; Hebrews 5:7). Let the weight of that truth sink in. When God himself, "who was tempted in every way that we are, except without sin" (Hebrews 4:15), walked the earth as one of us, he considered uninterrupted seasons of prayer to be essential for his earthly journey.

The bottom line is this: the FaithWalker who longs to live a story worth telling knows it simply can't be done without intentionally investing time for faith to find its voice in prayer.

Explore the Trail Ahead

You may not be carving out three hours to pray each day, as Martin Luther sometimes did. But you can take the next steps to investing more time in focused prayer.

- James 4:2 says that we have not because we ask not. As you've read this book and considered the state of your faith, what do you think you should be asking of God? Write down a list of the specific requests and commit to praying for them daily until God answers.

- It has been said that whatever doesn't get scheduled doesn't get done. Do you plan time for prayer? Consider scheduling time for prayer—even if it's five minutes to start. Then begin expanding that time in length and frequency.

- When was the last time you took a retreat to fast and pray about an issue you faced or a life decision you needed to make? Maybe it's time to plan an afternoon, evening, or weekend to hang out with God. Just talk, then listen.

Some of us are afraid to pray because we just don't know much about it. Consider beginning by reading The Complete Works of E. M. Bounds on Prayer. *It is an easy-to-read collection sure to expand your vision for the power of prayer.*

7

FAITH ANSWERS THE CALL

Kevin and Christina Quist were living the American Christian's dream. They lived with their five teen and preteen children in small-town Ohio where they taught at a private Christian high school. Kevin taught math and coached basketball; Christina taught English and communications while leading a girl's Bible study. All the kids played sports. Add driver's education, homework, friends, church activities, and all the rest, and, as with many families, their lives were ridiculously full. But their hearts were empty.

Christina described it this way in an interview with my friend Jeremy Statton:

> Our souls had been discontent for about four years.
> We felt restless, displaced. We were doing everything
> we were "supposed" to be doing, yet doing nothing
> at all. We would read about underground churches
> in China, people who were martyred for Jesus. We
> became so jealous of their faith. They knew Jesus in

a fierce, life-giving way. We knew Him in a comfortable, 90-minutes-on-Sunday way.

So, we read and prayed and pleaded and wrestled and—on a whim—e-mailed an organization called Living Hope to see if we could visit South Africa for two weeks. As it turned out, they were looking for someone to start a sports ministry and to work with teens through discipleship. It seemed like more than just a coincidence that they needed someone to do exactly what we were already good at.

In 2011, in a move that scared their parents half to death, the Quists stepped out in faith and answered the call. They quit their secure jobs, sold everything that wouldn't fit into a suitcase, and bought seven one-way tickets to Cape Town, South Africa—a place where pain is palpable. But that is what drew their hearts to that location: the injustice. Christina explained,

> The people there are forced to live in one sector of a
> beautiful city within shacks made of tin, no running
> water, house built upon house, crime and sickness
> rampant....But when we go to Masi for a game of
> pick up soccer, and I see my kids playing with kids
> with no shoes and dirty feet, I think, *This is how we
> should have been living all along....*On many levels,
> we need Africa more than it needs us.

In 2014, they answered the call to launch a nonprofit tutoring and guidance center for learners in Masiphumelele and Ocean View to combat unequal educational opportunities. Since then, they have partnered with existing organizations to coordinate their efforts. Their vision is to offer a caring place where students can come for academic help, counseling for drug and alcohol addictions, and mentoring for life. Their mission is clear: throw a wrench into the cycle of racism, poverty, and crime as they continue to walk by faith.

In two years, my friends Kevin, Christina, and their five teenage children have seen God move miraculously, both to provide and to open doors for ministry in ways they never imagined. These small-town Ohio family members now know and love their African "slum township" neighbors so much they can't even call it a slum. Because it is home. Christina reflects on the direction of their adventure thus far:

> Just [as] He walked with us in the beginning, God continues to walk with us now as we answer His call. We are absolutely floored that we have the opportunity to spread joy and love to people. If we, knowing hope, will risk everything to share hope with others, doesn't that make life worth living? We spent the first nineteen years of our marriage trying to polish the exterior of a shallow faith. *We want to live the next nineteen answering the call to live with abundant faith.*

Now that is a story worth telling. And it all began when their faith answered God's call.

WHAT YOUR RESPONSE REVEALS

Faith focused on God stands vigilant, poised to answer his call to travel across the world or walk across the room.

Depending on the circumstances, either one can be terrifying. And like Abraham, your calling may require you to step out without knowing all the details.

Perhaps the most basic truth is that a calling requires a caller, a person with whom you have a relationship. How you answer the call reveals your relationship with the caller. Think about it: if a stranger invited you to relocate your family to South Africa, you'd politely decline and keep walking without a second thought. But if a close friend from childhood called today and asked you to help start a school for orphans, you'd probably give it serious thought. You may not go, but you would treat the call differently because of the depth of your relationship.

So it is with God. When we have little to no relationship with him, we find it easy to ignore his call. We dismiss his tugging at our hearts because we don't recognize his voice. And our faith doesn't have the strength to listen because it isn't thriving on his Word or finding its voice in prayer. When we have no communion with God, we hear no calling from God.

When we invest time in relationship with him, however, we get to know and trust his character. As A. W. Tozer noted, "True faith rests upon the character of God and asks no further proof than the moral perfections of the One who cannot lie. It is enough that God has said it." It is in only while walking in close relationship with God that we can discern the direction he desires for our story. Unfortunately, we often choose our own direction—or allow someone else to choose it for us—and then assume God will approve.

Some years ago, the mayor of Cleveland, Ohio, came up with an idea to raise funds for her cash-strapped city. She offered citizens of the blue-collar bastion a chance to sponsor—a garbage can. For a small donation, you or your business could have your name emblazoned on a garbage can placed strategically around the city. It would still be a smelly trash receptacle, but it would have your name on it! Just donate and you could slap a sponsor sticker right on the front. As you might expect, the plan didn't meet with success, and the mayor moved in a different direction to generate cash flow. We might shake our heads, but this basic idea is a popular one in the church today.

We do what we want, then just slap a "Sponsored by God" sticker on it. We drift into whatever works at the moment and assume God's approval. We need a paycheck, so we take the job—and apply the label of God's provision. We're lonely, so we hang out with whoever will have us—and claim divine providence. We feel left behind, so we buy a better television, faster boat, or bigger house—and thank God for his "blessings." And then we struggle to figure out why our story just doesn't feel as if it's worth telling anymore. After all, it's got God stickers all over it.

But God's calling could never be contained on a sticker. It's a unique, one-of-a kind expedition, never quite what you expected, but always infinitely better than what you had planned. Take a moment now to consider what kind of stickers you may have used to decorate your story.

 ## CHECK YOUR COORDINATES

- Do you sense a dissatisfaction with your present vocation that you can't quite explain?

- Have you ever responded to a prompting from God in a way that seemed crazy to others?

- How much of your time is invested doing what you truly believe God has called you to do?

TEN STEPS FAITH CAUSES YOU TO TAKE

Once your faith is focused on what God wants, it moves you to respond to his call. When everyone else thinks it's impossible to walk on water, you get out of the boat and stroll because you know God's promises are sure and certain. You can see them there, just beneath the surface of life's waves. You step out as boldly as if you were walking out your front door. You don't step into nothing and hope for firm ground; you step onto God's promises and walk. Have you made any of these ten steps by faith?

1. **Step out of your comfort zone.** Just as Peter's faith moved him to step out of the boat, your faith will always call you to grow. And growth, by definition, is often uncomfortable. Remember that those who made it to the Faith Hall of Fame in Hebrews 11 did so in spite of intense discomfort. That is not to say that all discomfort looks the same. One person's challenge is another's disaster; but from God's perspective, there are no disasters—only opportunities to show himself strong on your behalf.

2. **Step up to challenges.** Scripture tells us, "If you show

yourself weak on a day of distress, your strength is too small" (Proverbs 24:10). Put positively, your strength can grow *exponentially* if you step up to the challenge. Try it, and you'll discover that the secret to the most explosive growth is to lean into, not away from, what challenges you the most.

3. **Step into messy situations.** Jesus stepped into the life of a hurting Samaritan woman by the well, much to the surprise of his temple-frequenting disciples (John 4). If God's mission is to bring hope to the hopeless, don't be surprised if his call requires you to love those most deem unlovable. As Mother Teresa reminds us, "Not all of us can do great things. But we can do small things with great love."

4. **Step over obstacles.** We all face barriers to answering the call. But God knew about those obstacles before he called you to live this story. The Apostle John described the resistance we encounter as being of the world and says, "This is the victory that has defeated the world: our faith" (1 John 5:4). We can offer excuses and pious apologies for disobedience, or we can take God at his Word and step over the obstacles in faith.

5. **Step past your failures.** J. M. Barrie clarifies a key truth: "We are all failures—at least the best of us are." If we are to grow, we must first embrace what we learn from failure as the only pathway to success. The writer of Proverbs says that the righteous person "may fall seven times but still get up" (Proverbs

24:16). The Apostle Paul called all FaithWalkers to follow his lead and forget what lies behind so they can "reach out for the things ahead....The goal [we] pursue is the prize of God's upward call in Christ Jesus" (Philippians 3:13-14). And if anyone could know about leaving the past behind, it's the guy who murdered Christ-followers for a living before faith opened his eyes!

6. **Step onto the promises of God.** When our faith is focused on God, we know that no foundation is more solid than God's promises. The Apostle Peter boldly portrayed them as our source for, well, everything: "By his divine power the Lord has given us everything we need for life and godliness....He has given us his precious and wonderful promises, that you may share the divine nature" (2 Peter 1:3-4). If you want a story worth telling for all eternity, step boldly into God's promises. Then hold on because your story is about to get good!

7. **Step behind others to support them.** Few can name the man whom the Apostle Paul said should be "show[n] great respect." Paul described Epaphroditus as the one who "serves my needs." He added, "He risked his life and almost died for the work of Christ" (Philippians 2:29, 25, 30). The Faith Hall of Fame is filled with ordinary people, not superstars. Sometimes the most significant step of faith can be placing yourself behind another who needs critical support.

8. **Step toward those who hurt.** It has been said that *hurt people hurt people.* Often the ones who need help the most resist our initial efforts to love them as Christ has loved us. But Jesus said, "When you give a banquet, invite the poor, crippled, lame, and blind. And you will be blessed because they can't repay you. Instead, you will be repaid when the just are resurrected (Luke 14:13-14). By loving those who can't return the favor, we ensure our story will be worth telling when it matters most.

9. **Step before anyone else moves.** Just as David was the first to run toward the blasphemous Goliath, the FaithWalker doesn't wait for his or her calling to be considered "cool." Because she believes, she leads—if that's what it takes. Leadership is just doing what you believe to be true in a way that inspires others to follow.

10. **Step down when the time is right.** After ten years at the helm of the Catalyst leadership conferences, my friend Brad Lomenick, author of *The Catalyst Leader*, stepped down when he sensed it was time for fresh perspective in the organization. As he described it to me, it was a choice that caused him to question his identity. Who would he be if not *the Catalyst-leader-guy*? But as Brad concluded, our identity must come from our relationship with the One who has called us, not from the task he has presently assigned to us.

PREPARE YOUR GEAR

Develop a Strengths Statement to Guide Your Calling

To get clear on your calling, you must identify your strengths. God has given you specific areas where you excel, where passion and talent unite to equip you to make a unique contribution. Although we can naturally sense these strengths, we don't always seek intentionally to cultivate them. These strength areas are generally where God will call us to live our story.

I took five years to drill down and develop the following strengths statement about myself:

I am at my best when I am creatively questioning, connecting, and communicating in the context of my beliefs.

That statement may not mean much to you, but it is powerfully clarifying for me. Do you know your strengths? Can you state them in a way that resonates with you?

HOW *NOT* TO IDENTIFY THE CALL

Let's face it: figuring out what God may be calling you to do can be downright confusing. Perhaps that's why so few Christians take the time to get clear on their calling. It can be a disorienting process, and the more clarity you get, the more trust is required. Of course, it is critical that your faith first be rightly focused on God, thriving on his truth, and finding its voice in prayer. Even then, the FaithWalker must continually rely on the Holy Spirit, who was sent to lead us into all truth (John 16:13). Those are just the prerequisites. Once you get into the actual journey of finding your calling, there are still a few hazards to avoid.

The life coach I mentioned earlier has become a dear friend. Dick Savidge specializes in creating unique opportunities for growth with Savidge Adventures (savidgeadventures.com). He showed me one danger that derails so many without their even noticing: along your journey to live a story worth telling, you will encounter great need, *but the need is not the call.* I am convinced—after counseling thousands, observing many more thousands, and examining my own life—that many Christians are not doing what God has called them to do. Instead, they are doing what others need them to do. Instead of being led by the Spirit of God, they are led by one urgent request after another. Yes, the needs are real. But being needed and being called are not the same things.

Consequently, our churches are full of Christians driven more by guilt than by calling, Christians choosing life direction not because they are convinced it is God's best but because they want to meet a need. But here's the truth: there will always be more needs than you could possibly meet. That's because you are not God. When we try to become God, we fail miserably, accomplish little, and live a story so scattered that the angels must struggle mightily to make sense of it.

We forget that even Jesus passed by countless needs in order to focus on his primary calling. As the Source of all wisdom, Jesus obviously understood what Jim Collins so famously penned in his book *Good to Great*: "Good is the enemy of great." Even as I write these words, I am reminded of at least six endeavors that could benefit from my involvement. Each of them is in need and each is advancing a worthy cause. But I am not called to help all of them, nor would it be wise for me to try to do so. That's not to say you should never help when needs arise. Rather choose what needs to meet based on God's calling for your life, not based on the frantic pleas of others. Understand that it is okay to say no. In fact, when we say no to a need because we are clear on our calling, we walk by faith, trusting that God has prepared someone who is better suited to meet that need.

On the other hand, sometimes God doesn't call us to something greater because we haven't proven our faithfulness where we are. During my dozen years as a leader at the school, there were times my gaze shifted ahead to how my calling might change. The founder and president of the school, Daniel Buell, offered wise counsel for those moments in the form of a baseball analogy: "You can only hit the pitch being thrown to you right now." We often look to the ninth inning, daydreaming about what we will do when we come to the plate then with bases loaded, two out, and a chance to be the hero. Meanwhile the early inning pitches blow by us unnoticed, and we're back on the bench, angry at the coach for depriving us of our big moment to shine later in the game. But if you were the coach, whom would you want in the game? Someone eagerly focused on his current assignment or someone lost in reverie about what may happen someday?

Jesus makes clear that if you are not faithful with the opportunity you have, don't expect to be given much more. Quite the opposite: expect what you have to be taken from you and given to someone who's proven to be more productive with the resources he or she has been given (Matthew 25:14-30). When it does come time for you to step away to a new calling, everyone you're leaving should miss you, not wish you had stopped whining and left long ago when you had clearly lost interest.

One final caution: sometimes we try to fulfill a need because we're afraid to tackle what we sense God really wants us to do. As I wrestled with the decision to follow God's call, I found myself rationalizing away the call with concern for how the school would fare if I left. I knew they needed me and that they would struggle greatly without me. And so I told myself that the need was just too great. Truth be told, I was afraid of stepping out. Somewhere along the way, the light came on. It was as if God said, "It's my school, not yours. If you are going to answer my call on your life, you've got to let *my* school go and trust me." Slowly yet firmly, God pried my fingers off the need (as well as my fear) so I could seize his call. I discovered firsthand how easy it is to identify a legitimate need, slap a God-sticker on it, and label it our "calling," when nothing could be further from the truth.

PARALYZED AT THE CROSSROADS

If you're like me, you've stubbed a few toes trying to figure out the specifics of what God wants for your adventure. I'm not talking about moral decisions on which God's Word is already clear. It's that gray area that can paralyze us: Should I go to college? If so, which one? Should I get married and if so, to whom?

Should I quit my job? Start a ministry? A business? Serve on the local zoning board? What career path is best? What church should I join? Do I buy a new car, a used car, a bicycle? Where should I live? What house should I buy, or do I rent? When do I sell? But where do I go and when?

I've found that the real concern I have in making these non-moral decisions is that I'm afraid I'll get it wrong. It's as if I think God has a perfect plan for my life that he's not sharing with me. One young man from my discipleship group put it this way: "I just want to be sure I am making the most of what God is giving me so I'll be pleasing to him." Awesome! I think most Christians would agree. But the same desire to live a story worth telling is one that can paralyze us into doing nothing if we don't ask the right questions.

Over my years on this faith adventure, I've learned to ask five questions when facing decisions about discerning God's direction for my life. There's nothing magical about these questions, but they are packed with trail-tested wisdom proven to bring clarity when making most of life's nonmoral decisions:

1. Do I Truly Want What God Wants?

Our *why* will determine our *what* and our *how*. If we seek his good first, God has promised to take care of the rest (Matthew 6:33). Often, we're disguising what we want as what God wants, slapping that God-sticker on it. Yet deep down we know the truth.

Only you can know your motives with any certainty. But instead of assuming you have the best ones, start by admitting that your desires are often less than the best, and pray the counterintuitive prayer of John the Baptist: "He must increase and I must decrease" (John 3:30). *Up* is *down* in God's story. John Maxwell captured this truth with the Law of Sacrifice: "You must give up to go up." God exalts those who humble themselves but resists those who exalt themselves. Don't be that person. Start with surrender. Only by losing your life to him can you ever hope to truly find it (Matthew 16:25).

2. Do I Know What I Want?

Once you've gotten clear on what God wants, you'll find that he often gives you great freedom to pursue what you want. But most of us never really take the time to figure it out, not clearly, anyway. Because we've never tackled the challenge of drilling down into what we really want and why, we aim at nothing in particular, then get frustrated when we achieve nothing in particular. Get clear on *what* you want before you decide *how* to get it.

3. Am I Asking for Wisdom?

According to Proverbs, wisdom is the "principal thing" (Proverbs 4:7 NKJV) and it is available to all who ask for it *by faith* from the God of all wisdom (James 1:5-7). But it's one thing to ask; it's another to seek it like hidden treasure (Proverbs 2:1-6). Are you asking for wisdom with fervent, focused prayer, or just casually mentioning it when you suddenly remember?

Wisdom isn't about checking the box and walking away; wisdom flows from a dynamic relationship with the God of all wisdom. Likewise, the Word of God promises to be a lamp to your feet and a light to your path, but not if you never read it. The

Holy Spirit was sent to "guide you in all truth" (John 16:13), but are you patiently listening?

4. Am I Getting Wise Counsel?

Most of us know we should get advice. However, we stack the deck of advisers to favor the choice we want to make in the first place. I've seen this more obviously in teens who consult their peers for advice on whether they should heed their parents' instruction. (That's one of those already decided moral issues, by the way.) But we adults do the same thing. We try to get our desires rubber-stamped by our peers instead of truly seeking advice we may not enjoy receiving. It's when we seek a wide array of counsel from those who have *been there, done that* that we get clarity on our true options. There truly is safety in counselors (Proverbs 11:14).

5. Do I Have All the Facts?

What you don't know *can* hurt you. All of us have made decisions based on what we thought we knew, only to find out later that our information was wrong. When Mary stood at the empty tomb and accused the "gardener" of stealing Christ's body, she thought she had all the facts (John 20:15). She was wrong. When Peter drew his sword in the garden, he obviously trusted his assessment of the situation (John 18:10-11). But he was wrong. When we don't know what we don't know, we're in deep trouble.

Turn over a few rocks. Dig deeper. Do your due diligence. Make your decision based on verifiable facts instead of on what you hope will happen.

Taking the time to answer these five questions thoroughly, will help you position yourself to discern God's direction for your life. Yes, you will leave some options behind. No, you can't have it all. Yes, you might need to adjust the plan later. No, not everyone will be happy with your choices. Answering the call of God in your story will involve risk. It will mean stepping out, even after you've done your homework, into the unclear or the unknown. That's why you need faith in the first place. What you see, sense, and feel won't always line up with what you believe to be true.

And, no, you cannot fulfill God's calling on your own. George Müeller stated it matter-of-factly: "Faith does not operate in the realm of the possible. There is no glory for God in that which is humanly possible. Faith begins where man's power ends."

So stop looking for God to reveal the future with a floodlight and remove all risk from your life. Start looking to God's character and promises to empower you to take righteous risks for his name's sake. Once you've pushed through the uncertainty to find clarity on your calling, as did the Quists mentioned at the beginning of the chapter, all that remains is to do the courageous thing: start walking in the new direction, and live a story worth telling.

EXPLORE THE TRAIL AHEAD

- Which of the ten steps in this chapter do you sense you need to take in your life right now? Write down what it is and what you can do this week to begin walking out your faith in that area.

- Do you know your strengths? When I began to intentionally explore my God-given abilities, I discovered I had strengths I didn't even recognize. Here are three resources from Marcus Buckingham that I used to identify my strengths:
  * Marcus Buckingham, *The Truth About You: Your Secret to Success* (Thomas Nelson, 2008)—a practical toolkit with book, DVD, and notepad.
  * Marcus Buckingham and Donald Clifton, *Now, Discover Your Strengths* (New York: The Free Press, 2001). Contains code for Strengthsfinder online assessment. Also see Tom Rath, *Strengthsfinder 2.0* (New York: Gallup Press, 2007).
  * Marcus Buckingham, *StandOut* (Nashville: Thomas Nelson, 2011). Terrific tool for discovering how your strengths mesh with others on a team.

- Once you've gotten clear on your strengths, you may still find it challenging to identify God's calling and the direction for your story. Here are three resources that may be helpful in understanding how God calls— and how we might respond:
  * Kevin DeYoung, *Just Do Something: A Liberating*

Approach to Finding God's Will (Chicago: Moody
Publishers, 2009).

* Os Guiness, *The Call* (Nashville: Thomas Nelson,
2003).

* John C. Maxwell, *Put Your Dream to the Test*
(Nashville: Thomas Nelson, 2009).

• Whenever you are contemplating a change in life
direction, talk to a wide range of people about what
that path requires, the demands it places on a family,
the potential rewards, and the price that must be paid
to succeed. Write down the names of at least three advisors on your FaithWalkers team who can help you
discern God's direction for your story.

Faith Moves You to Move Mountains

It was nearly nightfall when Moses looked out over the trembling waters of the Red Sea, took a deep breath, and held it. There it was, exactly where God said it would be. Moses stood, staring for a moment, as if expecting the watery barrier to fade like the many mirages he'd seen in the desert for decades while tending sheep. *Now I have sheep of a different kind to worry about*, the fledgling leader thought. He exhaled slowly while turning toward the teeming masses—nearly two million people—that stretched as far as he could see. They had cheered him just a few days ago as they followed him out of Egypt, but they weren't cheering now. Their furious, frustrated cries washed over him yet again. They clamored, complained, accused, and threatened to desert him. *They're just afraid*, Moses thought, an emotion he understood only too well.

As he continued his pivot away from the sea, he saw what the people saw behind them: the mightiest army in the world.

The Egyptian host stood ready to recapture or destroy them, whichever came easiest. He could see them only vaguely now, for they were blurred by the flaming cloud that had descended between them earlier that day. As the daylight faded quickly, Moses could see the flames more distinctly, an inferno sent by God himself to separate them from the Egyptians bent on vengeance.

Encouraged by the vivid reminder of God's intervention, Moses shook his head as if to clear it of fear and focus his faith on the One who had appeared to him in that burning bush. It felt so long ago, so far away. And yet, in spite of the bleak scenario, he could not shake the same sense he had felt then: God was up to something. Even now, in his darkest hour yet, he could feel it.

God is about to move, Moses thought, *if only we have the faith to follow.*

The obstacles he faced now—the sea in front, the army behind, and a mob all around—might as well have been the same mountains that had surrounded him that day he'd first encountered God while alone in the wilderness. Those mountains hadn't stopped him then, and somehow he doubted these barriers would stop God's people now. The sea and the army sure looked imposing, even insurmountable, but he had seen enough amazing miracles to know God was bigger.

Moses held his arms out beside him, palms upward, and lifted his face expectantly toward the starry sky and muttered, "I guess you know that I'm out of options here, God. If you're going to move, now would be a good time."

WHEN WE PUT GOD TO THE TEST

It's difficult to imagine a more challenging situation than the one Moses encountered that night at the Red Sea. We'll revisit the scene in a moment to learn how God responded to his plea. Moses' predicament may sound familiar to you: perhaps you have faced—or are facing—what appear to be impossible obstacles, mountains that threaten to keep you from answering God's call to live a story worth telling. The good news is that mountains make ideal settings for the best stories.

The disciples faced mountains too. You may recall one story we explored already on this journey to uncover how to live a story worth telling. The disciples had tried and failed to heal a demon-stricken boy, and Jesus had rebuked them for their lack of faith after healing the boy himself. This time, we'll turn our attention to what Jesus said to them. He stated a truth about moving mountains that is so incredible, it's often either misunderstood or dismissed as unbelievable:

> Then the disciples came to Jesus in private and asked, "Why couldn't we drive it out?"
>
> He replied, "Because you have so little faith. Truly I tell you, if you have faith as small as a mustard seed, you can say to this mountain, 'Move from here to there' and it will move. Nothing will be impossible for you." (Matthew 17:19-20 NIV)

"Nothing will be impossible for you [if you have faith]." And Jesus doesn't even require that much! For those unversed in agriculture, a mustard seed is one of the smallest of seeds. Jesus claims that when it comes to faith, size does not matter. Remember faith is really God's work in us, so he can turn many a willing heart into a mountain-moving muscle.

But Jesus is *not* saying that faith is a clever trick to get whatever you want. This verse is often contorted to mean that you can have whatever you desire, if only you believe. I've also heard it misconstrued to mean that God promises to deliver you from all ills, if only you believe. What results from such interpretations is a lot of sincere Christians who feel extremely guilty when they don't get what they want or find the healing they desire. Because the mountain they faced failed to move, they presume it was due to their lack of faith. After all, they did slap a God-sticker on it.

Such guilt-inducing interpretations of Scripture ignore the context in which Jesus gave this mind-blowing truth. First, his words were spoken privately to his disciples, not publicly to the masses. Second, the disciples were being groomed not to impress friends with their geological prowess, but to advance God's mission of reconciliation through faith in Christ. God's promises always presume God's purpose. Given the context in which Jesus spoke, the disciples would have understood it to mean something like this: "You could not fulfill my mission in this instance because you did not have faith. But when you do have faith when carrying out my mission, nothing will be impossible for you—not even moving mountains."

It might be helpful to recall that Jesus never actually *did* move any mountains. Why not? The success of his mission apparently did not require it.

And that is where most modern Christians would be comfortable leaving the conversation. Many would smugly settle back into their pews, feeling pretty good about having successfully defended God's Word from misinterpretation. But they would stop short of believing what Jesus said: "Nothing will be impossible for you." *Nothing.* Not because you are awesome but because you trust in the One who is. Not because your faith is super-sized but because it is focused with laser-like intensity on the God who is mighty to save. Not because you can move mountains yourself, but because your faith moves God to move mountains on your behalf and for the good of his mission.

E. M. Bounds captures the challenge God gives us: "Men and women are needed whose prayers will give to the world the utmost power of God; who will make His promises to blossom with rich and full results. God is waiting to hear us and challenges us to bring Him to do this thing by our praying. He is asking us, to-day, as He did His ancient Israel, to prove Him now."

 ## CHECK YOUR COORDINATES

- What mountains are you facing right now that seem impossible to move?

- Do you find yourself adding qualifiers to God's promises?

- Why do you think God has asked you to test him by acting on his promises?

THE SECRET TO MOVING MOUNTAINS

When Moses faced seemingly insurmountable barriers to carrying out God's mission, God answered his cry. God's answer gives us a simple pattern by which our faith can move us to move mountains as well. God's instructions to Moses can be summed up in two parts:

1. Stand still and see my salvation.
2. Keep moving forward.

Here's what Moses told the people as he received it from God, *and* how God responded to their needs:

> Moses said to the people, "Don't be afraid. Stand
> your ground, and watch the LORD rescue you today.
> The Egyptians you see today you will never ever see
> again. The LORD will fight for you. You just keep
> still."
>   Then the LORD said to Moses, "Why do you cry out
> to me? Tell the Israelites to get moving. As for you, lift
> your shepherd's rod, stretch out your hand over the
> sea, and split it in two so that the Israelites can go into
> the sea on dry ground." (Exodus 14:13-16)

Wait. What?! Stop *and* go? God's instruction to Moses would seem to be counterintuitive, even contradictory. Stand still *and* move forward at the same time? Yes, at the same time, but not in the same way. The faith required to move mountains calls us to *let go* but not to *let up*. Maybe an illustration would help.

GOD'S COUNTERINTUITIVE CALL

As we wrapped up the sale of our house and the calendar pages turned toward moving day, we faced the reality that, as of July 7, we would be homeless. We did not have another place to go, nor did we have much money with which to get there. Although we were confident God had called us to Atlanta, we didn't have any stable income lined up yet. The proceeds from the sale of our home would give us a few months' rent, we hoped, but that was it. Yet in the midst of this chaos, opportunities arose for me to write and fulfill my calling. Here's how I described the situation to a good friend at the time:

> I feel as if I am being asked to sit in the middle of a road at the bottom of a hill with steep mountains on either side. As I look up, there is an eighteen-wheel tractor trailer barreling down the hill toward me. It has no brakes. There is no way for it to avoid hitting me, and I could never outrun it. There is nothing I can do but sit in the middle of the road and wait. But God has handed me paper and pen; he has asked me to write. And he has promised that if I will ignore the truck barreling toward me and keep creating for his purposes, then he will save me from what seems to me to be certain destruction.

And so, to the best of my ability, that is what I did. I stopped trying to do God's work for him by scheming and manipulating the situation and instead focused on faithfully writing and creating as he had called me to do, while still moving forward toward Atlanta. My wife began packing. I reached out to help friends in and around Atlanta through various writing and creative projects. We even had a garage sale to thin out our stuff. By letting go of what we could not control but not letting up where we did have clear direction, we positioned ourselves for God to move a mountain on our behalf and for the good of his mission. We discovered, as the Hebrews did at the Red Sea, that God already had a solution in mind—we just didn't know what it was yet.

I'll share the rest of our story in a moment, but the solution God had in mind for the Hebrews removed both obstacles: opening the Red Sea *and* destroying the Egyptian army. It was an option far beyond anything Moses and the panicking Hebrews ever imagined. But then what would we expect from the One "who is able to do far beyond all that we could ask or imagine" (Ephesians 3:20)? Likewise, the solution God had in store for us came out of nowhere, but it would not have even been an option had we not remained diligent in the meantime, moving forward in the midst of tremendous uncertainty.

BE STILL AND KNOW

God's first instruction to the Hebrews was "Stand your ground." We might easily think, *With the Egyptians behind and the Red Sea in front, what other option did they have?* Evidently, God thought they needed to be told to stop their panicked flailing and just stand still. Think of how you react when you face a mountain, some unexpected obstacle that threatens to throw your world into chaos. Don't you try to come up with some way around it, over it, under it—anything to make it go away as quickly as possible? The problem is, our frantic, faithless efforts are just like those of a panicked drowning swimmer, making it nearly impossible for God save us in the way he most loves to.

The truth is that you will never see God's salvation until you stop trying to save yourself. This is why the psalmist famously called us not to fear but to "be still" when surrounded by the chaos of life (Psalm 46:10 NKJV). When we reach for anything and everything within our power to fix it ourselves, we usually only make it worse. Abraham thought he could solve his problem of not having an heir by reaching for Hagar, but he didn't get Isaac. He got Ishmael and the beginning of thousands of years of conflict between their descendants (Genesis 16). We're best positioned to see God move mountains when we stop trying to move them ourselves.

It is only when we stop trying to do God's work for him that we can "see the salvation of the LORD" (Exodus 14:13 NKJV) or as the psalmist put it, "know that [he is] God" (Psalm 46:10 NKJV). The Hebrew word translated "know" contains the idea of knowing *by observing*. In other words, "Be still and know who I am by watching me work." God doesn't move mountains for you when you're already trying to move them in your own way. To put it another way, you are not God's opening act. The psalmist records God as stating the obvious that we often forget: "I will be exalted among the nations, I will be exalted in the earth!" (Psalm 46:10 NKJV). God created us to delight in watching him do what only he can do. When we trust God enough to stand down, we invite his power to show up.

But that doesn't mean God will show up on our schedule. I'm

sure Moses would have preferred God open the Red Sea sooner. And I know I would have been happy to get the details of our move to Atlanta sometime *before* we moved out of our house. But the story could not so wondrously reveal the majesty of God if we had not been so radically dependent on him. God shows his greatness best when our situation can't get much worse. The psalmist declared that God would save us "just at the break of dawn" (Psalm 46:5 NKJV). He loves to wait until we are out of options so there can be no mistaking who is responsible for the solution. It should not surprise us when God waits until just before morning comes to deliver us. In fact, we should expect it.

PREPARE YOUR GEAR

When Is It Okay to Ask God Why?

Every FaithWalker has been there: standing in front of a mountain that doesn't seem to be moving. In those frustrating times, few of us dare to ask God the question we really want to ask: Why? The truth is that why? *can be the perfect question to increase your faith if you're asking for the right reason.*

Here are three questions to discern your motive for asking why *of the Almighty:*

- **Are you accusing God?** Your questions can be cover for complaints. The Israelites mastered this approach. They didn't really want answers. They wanted to throw verbal stones. "But the people were very thirsty for water there, and they complained to Moses, 'Why did you bring us out of Egypt to kill us, our children, and our livestock with thirst?' " (Exodus 17:3). This self-centered approach never worked well for them and it won't for you.

- **Are you confused by events?** When your walk of faith takes an unexpected turn, you can become disillusioned. In such instances, the problem is not with God but with your expectations. If you begin to write the story for him, you may get confused when he erases your hurried sketches to replace them with a masterpiece of his own design.

- **Are you genuinely wanting to learn?** Sometimes, the best question that forms wisdom is *why?* There's nothing wrong with asking God honest questions when you truly want to know how to become a better FaithWalker. Just prepare yourself for the answer, because "My plans aren't your plans, nor are your ways my ways, says the LORD" (Isaiah 55:8).

GOD MOVES OUR HOUSE-SIZED MOUNTAIN

When July 7 arrived, our kids moved in with my in-laws while my wife and I headed to Atlanta to look for a house. After almost a year with no income, we didn't have enough money to actually purchase a house of our own. But we chose to keep moving forward and look anyway, because I had some promising connections in Atlanta, and we had begun a conversation with a family member about partnering to purchase a house there. Once again, we followed Abraham's lead and went out, not knowing where we were going.

We scheduled a full three days of house viewings, but as it turned out, the very first house we saw was the only one that made sense for our family. There was just one little problem. The current owners wanted actual money—and we didn't have much. So we prayed. We informed the potential family partner of our find and then waited.

With God's instructions to Moses echoing in our hearts, we intentionally chose not to try to manipulate the situation to make it happen. We presented the facts and then did our best to get out of God's way. We even went to see a movie, knowing that if God didn't make a way to purchase that house, we'd return to Ohio, regroup, and come back to search for a rental. We waited, palms open upward, expecting God to make his move, hoping that his move wouldn't involve living in a cardboard box beneath an overpass.

And then God moved the mountain, just at the break of dawn. The family member agreed to partner with us on the purchase. We went through the usual process, and twenty-five days later we moved into a beautiful house near Atlanta that far exceeded anything we could have imagined. We had stood still *and* kept moving forward with what light we had. And he had saved us, just at the break of dawn.

But if God had chosen another path for us, one that included a cardboard box or a longer delay, his promise to provide for our needs would still be valid. The mountain might have moved differently or on a slower timetable, but it would still be a story celebrating his faithful provision, just the same. That's just how God rolls.

MOUNTAINS CAN BE FUNNY THINGS

One thing I've learned along my journey is not to make assumptions about mountains. For one thing, mountains are not always what they appear to be. When the Hebrews faced the Red Sea, they thought it an impassable barrier. It wasn't. When we were homeless and without money, buying a house seemed impossible. Not so.

I mentioned my friend Daniel Buell earlier, founder of Cornerstone Christian Academy in Willoughby Hills, Ohio, where I had served. He too faced a seemingly impossible task in the summer of 2000 when he agreed to lead the effort to launch and open a college-prep school for grades 7 to 12—in less than two months! At the time, only eleven students were enrolled, I was the only teacher with a contract, and the school had not yet been chartered by the state of Ohio. Anyone with any experience in education will tell you that these barriers Dan faced were insurmountable. Perhaps with an additional year—and a lot of money—the task could be done. Maybe.

But Dan persisted by faith, believing that God had called him to run toward the seemingly impossible to establish a vibrant Christian school for God's glory. He built a dedicated team quickly and spent a lot of nights in the office, watching the sun come up on yet another stack of completed paperwork. Nothing came easily. But incredibly, when the first bell rang, the school opened with full faculty, an enrollment of 131, and state-charter status in record time—an accomplishment that was nothing less than a bureaucratic miracle. Today the school is thriving. It consistently enrolls nearly four hundred students annually in grades K–12 and sends graduates to the best colleges and universities throughout the nation. Where most saw impossibility, Dan saw something different: opportunity. Here's his perspective: "A mountain is merely a change in the terrain you must travel, so keep hiking."

And that's the other funny thing about mountains. From God's perspective, there are none. You may have heard the expression that someone is "making a mountain out of a molehill," making a big deal about something that is truly insignificant. We all too easily forget that God sees no mountains, only molehills. If we can remember God's perspective as we answer his call to live a story worth telling, we can patiently be still and watch him work, like Moses, even while we keep moving forward by faith.

EXPLORE THE TRAIL AHEAD

- Think of someone you know who has faced what you think is a mountain and overcome it by faith. Ask him or her to share the story with you. It may be just the encouragement you need to face the barriers in your own life.

- Have you ever put God to the test before and seen him move unmistakably to provide? If so, write down a brief account of that chapter in your story and share it with someone in need of encouragement today.

- What mountains do you see when you think about pursuing the dreams God has planted within you? Name each of them. Now ask God for the wisdom to identify the first steps you can take to climb those mountains (or move them). You may want to consider fasting as you focus your prayers on asking God to do the impossible through you.

- Think of the mountains you have identified. Are they barriers to what God has called you to do or to what *you* want to do? Ask God to reveal to you the hidden motives of your heart. Remember: God's promises always presume God's purposes.

9

FAITH KEEPS MOVING FORWARD

Glenn Cunningham didn't even want to go outside that frigid February morning in 1916. The eight-year-old boy reluctantly made the two-mile trek with his older brother to the one-room schoolhouse. The first ones to arrive, they took the initiative to get the school warmed by starting a fire. But as his brother lit the coal stove with kerosene as usual, Glenn thought something didn't smell quite right. When he realized the can wasn't full of kerosene at all he turned to shout a warning. But he was too late.

A second later, the gasoline can left carelessly by the stove exploded with a blinding flash, hurling Glenn to the floor. He dimly heard his brother scream, "I'm on fire!" Then Glenn realized that he was, too. The two panicked boys plunged their bodies into the snow outside before running for home, their skin still burning and peeling away as they staggered in shock across the two miles of Kansas prairie—only to find no one home. Though help finally arrived, Glenn's brother was unable to recover from the burns and lost his battle for life a few weeks later.

Young Glenn was left lying helpless for months, praying for his charred legs to heal, although doctors offered little hope that he would ever walk again. But Glenn refused to give up the idea of walking, even if it meant moving forward through excruciating pain. His injuries forced him back to the basics. He began by dragging himself along the floor, his useless limbs trailing behind him. Then he leaned on a chair for support as he shifted his stubborn legs. Finally, nearly two years after the accident, Glenn took his first halting steps on Christmas morning. His father urged him forward, making the boy join him on errands, often in spite of his mother's worried protests. Glenn held the tail of the family horse, letting it pull him forward, forcing his legs to strengthen. By summertime, Glenn was walking again.

One leg would remain forever shorter than the other. And he would never rid himself completely of the chronic pain. But as Glenn leaned into the challenge, something amazing happened. His legs didn't just regain strength; they became stronger than most. His passion to walk became a hunger to run, all the time and everywhere, simply because he could. As he grew into a young man, it became clear that his commitment to keep moving forward had made him not just a good runner—but one of the fastest in the world.

More than a decade after that morning at the schoolhouse, Glenn found himself preparing for the 1932 Olympic Games, the early favorite to win a gold medal. Just days before the competition, though, a severe case of tonsillitis forced him to miss his race. Such a setback would have destroyed lesser men, but Glenn kept moving forward, refusing to quit. Four years later, he made the team again. This time, he ran—and won a silver medal in the 1936 Olympic Games in Berlin. Then he retired.

If that were the end of the story, it would be a good one. But God had even greater things in store for Glenn. After his retirement, Glenn used his fame and experience of forging forward through adversity to start a ranch to minister to troubled youth. His faith in God kept him focused on moving forward for God's mission. By the time of his death in 1988, more than nine thousand teens—all bearing scars of various types—had their stories altered by an encounter with the boy from Kansas who never quit.

THE PERILS OF MOVING FORWARD

When God told Moses and the Israelites to keep moving forward toward the Red Sea, he was not telling them to do something easy. We often think that *easy* means *right* and *difficult* means *wrong*. There was nothing easy about young Glenn's battle to walk, and there was nothing easy about what God asked the Hebrews to do that night at the Red Sea—but both instructions were right and good.

Picture yourself as the typical Hebrew at the Exodus. Your last few weeks have been an emotional roller coaster. First, this guy emerges from the wilderness and says he's been sent by God to free your people after four hundred years of slavery. You dare to hope, but his first attempts just make life worse for you and your family. Over the next several weeks, you endure plagues of various sorts alongside the Egyptians as your hopes are repeatedly dashed when Pharaoh refuses to free you. Finally, after your most harrowing night, you leave behind the only home you've ever known and head into the wilderness—free at last!—only to run into what looks like a dead end. The Egyptian army is behind you, hidden behind a pillar of fire that looks downright dangerous. You pull your children closer as the darkness deepens, wondering if this night will be your last with them. And then you hear word passed along that this leader, who doesn't even speak very well, says God wants you all to walk toward the Red Sea.

It sounds crazy, but what have you got to lose? So that is exactly what you do. You start walking toward the water, surrounded by two million other Hebrews, your way lit only by the flickering flames hovering in the air behind you. And as you begin to move, what you can see, sense, and feel only gets worse. A gale-force wind begins whipping around you, sending sand into your mouth and eyes. You shield your face with one arm and reach frantically for your screaming children with the other, praying you don't get separated in the jostling crowd. You keep shuffling forward together in the dark for some time before you realize that you should have hit water by now. You work your way to one side, stumbling over boulders, thinking you must have gotten turned around. And then you look up.

You stare for a moment at the dark wall of swirling water, your mouth dropping open. You flinch as your youngest daughter screams in terror, then collapses completely, sobbing. You swallow hard and turn away from the watery wall to scoop up the wailing child. You take a quick glance backward at the mass of people pressing toward you and realize that the only way out now is forward. Reaching blindly for the rest of your family, you shuffle ahead into the darkness, feeling tugs on your robe that you hope signal the rest of your family following.

Clearly, what God called the Hebrews to do was anything but

easy. What makes us think our lives will be different? Maybe it's the Disneyesque expectation of a magical fairy appearing to deliver us from danger that creates this illusion. We mistakenly believe that "with God all things are possible" means that with God all things are trouble-free. Not true. Your journey to live a story worth telling will not be effortless. Jesus himself warned his disciples of difficulty: "In the world you have distress. But be encouraged! I have conquered the world" (John 16:33).

God doesn't promise easy. But he does promise to blow away your expectations *if* you have the courage to step toward the mountain he has called you to move. The test of your faith is discovering what it takes to stop you.

FAITH IN MOTION

Our natural inclination is to run from mountains, to flee from adversity, to take shelter when we see a storm brewing on the trail ahead. Challenges threaten to expose our limitations and leave us vulnerable, exposed as the fearful child that each of us is on the inside. But faith focused on God moves us to walk toward the mountain in spite of that fear, to lean into the challenge—not so we can be proven great, but so that God can reveal himself on our behalf. It is only when we first move toward the mountain that God moves. Our motion is evidence of our devotion.

My family saw this truth play out often in our journey to live a story worth telling. Not long after our income went to zero, I prayed a very specific prayer. When we had purchased our house several years earlier, the previous owner had left a large tractor, complete with a backhoe, in the backyard. We had never gotten it to start but knew that it could be worth something for parts to the right buyer. And so I began to pray earnestly that God would sell it before we put our house up for sale. We needed the money to pay the bills and, let's face it, rusty backhoes don't contribute much to curb appeal. I made some calls and gathered some interest. But then I got distracted. I traveled a bit, other stuff came up, and to my shame, I neglected fervent, focused prayer for the sale.

Finally, I confessed my sin of prayerlessness and refocused my efforts. It was Thursday morning when I began praying that God would sell the tractor for one thousand dollars and have it out of our yard by the end of that week. I confess that I simply couldn't see how God *could* answer. The tractor weighed more than six tons! It hadn't moved in four years, and I knew next to nothing about mechanical stuff. It would need to cross a rickety bridge to leave the yard, if we could find a way to move it at all. Plus someone would have to be willing to buy it for more than anyone had yet offered.

As I sat in the backyard, staring at the tractor and praying, I suddenly realized that if I really expected God to move that John Deere mountain of rust, I should start preparing for it. My gaze shifted to the bridge over which the tractor would have to travel. And I knew what I had to do: step into the waters of that muddy creek to brace that rickety bridge. And so I did.

The next day, the phone rang. The man on the other end of the line specialized in reclaiming old tractors and selling them for parts. If I could have the tractor across the bridge by Saturday, he would buy it—as is. I told him not to worry, the bridge was already braced. A little creativity and a lot of work later, the tractor inched across the bridge I had fortified in anticipation of God's answer.

By the end of the week, the tractor had left the yard for—you guessed it—one thousand dollars.

There seems to be a pattern here. When your faith in God moves you to move mountains, he almost always expects you to do something first. When he parted the waters of the muddy Jordan, he required the priests first to step into the waters. When he delivered King Jehoshaphat and the people of Judah from their enemies, they took the first step, filled with confident praise for God's coming deliverance:

> Early the next morning they went into the Tekoa wilderness. When they were about to go out, Jehoshaphat stood and said, "Listen to me, Judah and every inhabitant of Jerusalem! Trust the LORD your God, and you will stand firm; trust his prophets and succeed!"
>
> After consulting with the people, Jehoshaphat appointed musicians to play for the LORD, praising his majestic holiness. They were to march out before the warriors, saying, "Give thanks to the LORD because his faithful love lasts forever!" As they broke into joyful song and praise, the LORD launched a surprise attack against the Ammonites, the Moabites, and those from Mount Seir who were invading Judah, so that they were defeated. (2 Chronicles 20:20-22)

Likewise, when David faced Goliath, he did not decry the problem and pray for deliverance, as no doubt many others were already doing. He first ensured that removing the giant was in line with God's priorities and promises, then he selected five smooth stones, warmed up his sling, and ran confidently forward, expecting God to show up. And God showed himself strong on his behalf. When we run to answer God's call, obstacles become opportunities for God to reveal our faith. A lot of Christians talk a good faith game, but when it comes time to perform in the face of stiff resistance, they discover they don't have much faith at all. Confusing the easy way with God's way, we quit just when God's way is about to get good. The truth is that you'll never know if you really believe until you follow God to a place where you must act and trust that he will provide.

 ## Check Your Coordinates

- Have you ever encountered adversity that left you feeling as if God had forsaken you?

- Do you expect the journey to live a story worth telling to be easy?

- What are you attempting now for God that will fail if God does not come through?

Faith Is a Process

When we started on this journey together, I noted that faith is not so much an event as it is a process. Certainly it includes those one-time experiences where you make courageous decisions and encounter mountains that require moving. But more often, faith means moving forward slowly but surely, closing the gap between what we believe to be true and what we see, sense, and feel. One day, our faith will become sight. And faith will be no more. For faith itself is also a temporary thing, a necessary part of living a story worth telling in an environment where what we see, sense, and feel often contradicts what we know to be true. The resistance we meet in the process, and how we respond to it, prepares the way for the miraculous.

The Faith Process Reveals Our Faith to Us

When God instructed Abraham to sacrifice his son Isaac, the one through whom God's promises were to be realized (Genesis 22), it wasn't because God needed to see if Abraham had faith. God already knew. But Abraham didn't. Until that moment, only God knew to what extent Abraham would obey him. Likewise, God knew that Job's faith would stand, but Job didn't, and neither did the great deceiver who wanted so desperately to shake his faith. Sometimes God leads us into places where great faith is required in order to let us see just how much faith we have.

The Faith Process Enables Our Purification

As Peter preached in Acts 15:9, God cleanses our hearts by faith. It is a purifying tool he uses to remove sin and make us holy. Of course, this process of purification can be painful, gradual, and frustrating for us at times. But we can take comfort in knowing that the process is an intentional one, because "the one who started a good work in you" has promised to complete it (Philippians 1:6).

The Faith Process Makes Us Humble

God brings humility to you so he can do great things through you. God revealed his purpose in the Israelites' wilderness wandering in Deuteronomy 8:2: "Remember the long road on which the LORD your God led you during these forty years in the desert so he could humble you, testing you to find out what was in your heart: whether you would keep his commandments or not." Being humbled is not always enjoyable, but it is necessary to fully reveal the majesty of God.

The Faith Process Grows Our Faith Through Failures

Abraham's faith failures are well documented in Scripture. He falsely claimed his wife was his sister—twice (Genesis 12, 20). Because he struggled to believe that God would give him his promised son in the promised way, he had a son by his wife's servant. And yet, in spite of these failures and many others like them, the Apostle Paul describes him this way:

> Without losing faith, Abraham, who was nearly 100 years old, took into account his own body, which was as good as dead, and Sarah's womb, which was dead. He didn't hesitate with a lack of faith in God's promise, but he grew strong in faith and gave glory to God. He was fully convinced that God was able to do what he promised. (Romans 4:19-21)

Abraham's faith clearly did waver on numerous occasions, so why did Paul describe his faith in such glowing terms? The FaithWalker is not one who always walks perfectly, but the one who gets back up and keeps walking, even after failing miserably. As Paul said, Abraham "grew strong in faith" through a process that obviously included many failures. Yet he is not remembered for his failures, but for the faith process that moved him to more fully focus on God.

The Faith Process Tests God Even as It Tests Us

Through the prophet Malachi, God dared his people to take a step of faith by giving him a tithe offering:

> Bring *the whole tenth-part*
> *to the storage house*
> *so there might be food in my house.*
>
> *Please test me in this,*
> *says the* LORD *of heavenly forces.*
>
> *See whether I do not open*
> *all the windows of the heavens for you*
> *and empty out a blessing until there is enough.*
> *(Malachi 3:10)*

The testing of our faith and our faith's testing of God are different (because unlike our faith, God can't grow any stronger). God challenges us to walk by faith so he can have the opportunity to demonstrate his own faithfulness. When our faith fails to put God to the test, it's usually for one of two reasons: either we want to fix it ourselves, or we're afraid he might not be up to the task.

Whatever you are facing in life right now, the solution is to keep moving forward through the faith process, passing the test while putting God to the test. By fixing your eyes on Jesus, the author and finisher of your faith, you'll discover that the way out is forward, for that is the only way your life can truly become a story worth telling.

 PREPARE YOUR GEAR

Five Tips to Keep Moving Forward

1. **Check what you are *not* doing.** Make sure you are not trying to "help" God along by taking matters into your own hands.

2. **Check what you *are* doing.** Are you really doing all you can, or is God waiting for you to do something he has clearly led you to do? If you find you've neglected something, get busy.

3. **Focus on today.** Many FaithWalkers quit out of anticipation of the pain they might feel tomorrow. But the reality is that tomorrow seldom hurts as much as we think it will.

4. **Take one more step.** For the FaithWalker your faith is only as strong as your next step forward. So take one more step.

5. **Find friends.** You cannot make it alone. Not only do you need to rely on God, but you also need the support of other FaithWalkers. If you need help, don't be afraid to be very clear in asking.

When Nothing Is Easy

On this journey to live a story worth telling, you won't find many people with faith more firmly focused on God than Deborah and Branden Scattone—or people who've experienced a more challenging series of unfortunate events in the first twelve years of their marriage. Yet they keep moving forward, in spite of what they see—or in Deborah's case, do not see. For at the age of thirty-one, this mother of three daughters found herself suddenly blind. And that wasn't even the worst of it.

It started just three months before their wedding in 2003, when Deborah began feeling unusually tired. Within one week, her muscles ached so severely that she could no longer turn the steering wheel of her car. She was soon diagnosed with dermatomyositis, one of those conditions modern medicine has yet to fully unravel. It left her with ongoing inflammation of joints and severe muscle weakness; it also left her prone to acute skin irritations, especially when exposed to any sunlight. Medications soon brought the symptoms under control, until a year later when she learned she was pregnant with their first child. Because the medication also induced abortions, she stopped taking it to preserve the life of her new daughter. Incredibly, the pregnancy went well, and her condition seemed to stabilize after the birth.

At least it did until the next pregnancy in June 2006. Expecting to be excited at the news of a second child, Deborah and Branden discovered instead that the egg had failed to reach its destination in the uterus and was now growing elsewhere, a condition known as an ectopic pregnancy. Deborah's ovary then ruptured without her knowing it, causing internal bleeding that threatened her very life.

Following the failed pregnancy, Deborah plunged into deep depression that lasted for three months. She talked openly with Branden about the horrific dreams, suicidal thoughts, and what she describes as an evil presence that plagued her. Finally one night, amid inexplicable screams from her daughter and the darkest of thoughts bombarding her imagination, she rebuked in the name of Jesus whatever dark forces might be at work in their home and defiantly proclaimed, "You can't have me! You can't have my family!" Immediately, the sense of foreboding vanished and her depression subsided, never to return.

In the summer of 2007, the Scattones took a financial risk: they purchased several smaller rental properties. Initial results were positive, and they learned Deborah was pregnant once again. Christmas that year shone with hope for a bright future.

But three days later, Branden was diagnosed with colon cancer, a rare condition for someone so young. Over the next six months, Deborah was forced to continue to work full-time to make ends meet, often under challenging physical conditions, as Branden underwent evaluation, preparation, surgery, and recovery. Though his colon had to be removed, he survived and needed no colostomy bag—both miracles. So the couple kept moving forward, unwavering in their faith, eager to attempt more for God.

In the summer of 2008, three months after Branden's cancer surgery and six months into Deborah's pregnancy, they purchased a struggling pizza shop, hoping to turn it around. They were seeing signs that their rental properties were not all they had expected them to be. After six months of pouring themselves into the business night and day, they did make it a profitable endeavor, but at a high cost to their health and family well-being. Meanwhile, the housing market had collapsed, and they discovered they had been the victims of shady mortgage lending in the purchase of their rental properties. A buyer wanted to purchase the pizza franchise, but after agonizing over the offer, they chose to continue their harried pace. It was a decision they would soon regret.

Over the next six months, Deborah's health deteriorated rapidly. Finally, Branden insisted she stop working. Without her help, they were forced to sell the shop at a loss back to the franchiser and declare bankruptcy, losing not only the three rental properties but eventually their own home as well.

April 2011 saw a ray of hope in the midst of great disappointment—the arrival of their third daughter. But the delivery itself threw one of Deborah's hips out of joint, and she found herself unable to walk up stairs for six months. Then intense, unexplained head pain and nausea landed her in the emergency room. Perhaps it was the side effect of a new medication. No one ever knew for sure. But the pain continued to increase, and her ongoing condition of dermatomyositis flared up again with fresh vigor. Finally, one morning in October 2011, Deborah awoke and said simply, "I can't see." She was completely blind.

The intense pain and blindness made it an hour-plus ordeal to get Deborah into the car and on the way to the hospital. Three days, fifteen medications, and 3,000 mg of steroids later, she came home, but her eyesight had only partially returned.

Inflammation had completely detached both retinas. The doctors did not expect her ever to see again. There was no recourse but to pray that they would reattach themselves, so that's what Deborah and Branden did.

And after several months, the blackness began to fade into a blur—yet another miracle, according to the many doctors who examined her. Her healing was soon being discussed at medical conferences around the country. One doctor who could offer no explanation for her healing told her plainly, "I don't know." Deborah responded, "That's because you're not God."

Today, Deborah's sight is now restored nearly to normal with corrective lenses, although it fluctuates from day to day. The dermatomyositis has once again gone into remission, though she still has no idea what causes the intense pain in her legs from time to time or the nerve issues that seem to come and go without reason.

Yet after all of her family's challenges, you will not find a more consistently positive person than Deborah. When I asked her to describe the barriers she faces each day, she replied simply:

> I don't have any barriers. Every day I feel different.
> Every day I feel there's something different wrong
> with me. I live each day with the restraint that is
> there that day. So the days that I feel well, I'm out-
> side playing with the kids, making cookies, or doing
> crafts with them. When my days are bad, I just rest.
>
> We've learned that the word *can't* is not in God's
> vocabulary. We know that nothing is impossible for

him. I can see and the doctors said that was impossible. We've seen God move again and again. There are no barriers when your faith is focused on him.

She doesn't have this attitude because life is suddenly all better. At the time we talked, Branden was facing another digestive tract surgery. Deborah still can't drive or do much of anything physically; she can't even plan anything in advance because her health vacillates to such extremes. But her faith makes her outlook completely the opposite from what we would expect:

I've prayed for years to be home with my kids, but I would never, ever have quit my job. But now because of my unpredictable blindness, I am home with them and get to work with them each day, live life alongside them, fix meals when I can, and just pour into them. They'll remember these times. They'll remember the times when Daddy wasn't feeling well, but he went sledding with them anyways.

The first thing we get from people who hear our story is, "You're so young!" But we tell them in a way that makes it clear we believe God is working it for good, so they don't really question why. At least not to us. They see that we are still praising even though we're still struggling.

As for me, I never really asked God why. I used to ask, "Why *more?*" but I stopped. We don't think much about the past, about what we've gone through. We just live life with more awareness than

most people that we have little control over what
happens to us.

As we've seen with Glenn Cunningham and with Moses and
the people of Israel, the instructions are simple. Deborah Scattone said it best: "We focus our faith on God and keep moving
forward." So will you, as you pursue living a story worth telling.

EXPLORE THE TRAIL AHEAD

- Sometimes we bring hard times on ourselves by doing foolish or even sinful things that leave us with painful consequences. Be honest with yourself about the hard times you face right now. What is the result of walking by faith, and what is the result of poor decisions you have made? God can work with both, but only if you're honest with yourself about the cause.

- Continuing to move forward can feel too painful in the face of great loss or great adversity. If all you can do is stand still, start there for now. But ask God to increase your faith and look for the opportunity to take the next step forward—even if it's a small one.

- Do you tend to dwell on your faith failures? The FaithWalker is known not for always succeeding, but for getting back up again after failure and pressing on anyway. Failure has power over you only if you allow it. What failures do you need to let expire now?

- As you pray for God to answer specific requests, do you prepare for God's answers? Take a moment to jot down the requests that are on your heart most often. Next to each one, write down any actions you need to take to get ready for the answers. If you have done all you can, keep praying and expecting God to answer in his perfect timing.

10

FAITH CHANGES EVERYTHING

We all want our lives to become stories worth telling, yet every FaithWalker struggles with the pull of what he sees, senses, and feels. We'd be tempted to call this "reality" were it not for the unseen that we believe to be true. Fortunately for us, as Frederica Matthews-Green said, "Reality is God's home address." If we have the faith to see reality from his point of view, we gain fresh perspective on where, when, and why our story will be told.

We all share a desire to turn our lives into legend, stories that outlive us and contribute significantly to our posterity long after our brief tenure on this planet has ended. That's not a bad thing. It's certainly better than "Eat, drink and be merry, for tomorrow you may die." We recognize the truth that Moses wrote: "We live at best to be seventy years old, maybe eighty, if we're strong....They go by so quickly. And then we fly off" (Psalm 90:10). Life is short. And we know it. So we concern ourselves with building something that outlives our brief appearance on this earthly stage, hoping, as the poet Walt Whitman put it, to contribute a verse to the "powerful play."

Some call it *legacy*. As Benjamin Disraeli described, "The legacy of heroes is the memory of a great name and the inheritance of a great example." But memory can mislead, and greatness is open to interpretation. Only a handful of generations ago, the American Civil War claimed the lives of more than six hundred thousand soldiers who no doubt sought to be remembered. And yet few of us could name even five of those men. Even though many died heroically and each had a unique story, their memory has already faded for all but a few history buffs. No doubt Genghis Khan, Alexander the Great, and even Adolph Hitler all aimed for greatness and even hoped to be identified as heroes by future generations. Yet history views their stories differently than they may have hoped.

The truth is that we want to turn this temporary tale into something lasting, something permanent, something—dare we say it?—immortal. Some try to achieve this immortality through fame or political success. Others take the philanthropic course and donate billions to noble causes through charitable foundations. Still others, like the Romantic poets, hope to achieve immortality through art. But granite crumbles, and art fades a little more with each passing generation.

There is a tremendous irony in our rabid pursuit of immortality. When faith opens our eyes, we see that we are all, in God's reality, already immortal. And so is our story. C. S. Lewis penned these clarifying words: "You have never talked to a mere mortal. Nations, cultures, arts, civilizations—these are mortal, and their life is to ours as the life of a gnat. But it is immortals whom we joke with, work with, marry, snub and exploit—immortal horrors or everlasting splendors."

We are all already immortal. Not our physical bodies that we can see with our physical eyes, but our souls, the essence of who we are, can never die. From God's perspective, how futile all of our quests to achieve immortality through this temporary stuff must seem! We've got it all backward.

 CHECK YOUR COORDINATES

- How often do you think of yourself, and those around you, as immortal beings?

- How frequently do you consider the impact of your actions on generations that follow?

- If you could choose to be known for one thing, what would it be?

WHERE WILL YOUR STORY BE TOLD?

Faith focused on God makes your story worth telling because it opens your eyes to where and when your story will be told. Because of our fixation on "the seen," we tend to think only of the impact of our story in this brief season of our existence: the *here and now*. Although that impact is not unimportant, as immortal beings we should be far more concerned with how our story will sound when it is told *there and then*, in that next season of existence that will extend through all eternity.

Unfortunately, for many Christians, the goal is simply to get across the finish line after surviving this earthly life. Having been steeped in the Christian church culture for decades, I know it's challenging to break out of this finish-line mentality. Our fixation on that moment of passing from this life to the next is partly due to the reality that "we must all appear before the judgment seat of Christ" (2 Corinthians 5:10 NKJV). It's also partly due to our emphasis on the metaphorical language the biblical writers used to describe our time on earth, the language of running a race:

- "Let's also run the race that is laid out in front of us." (Hebrews 12:1)
- "I have fought the good fight, finished the race, and kept the faith." (2 Timothy 4:7)
- "Don't you know that all the runners in the stadium run, but only one gets the prize? So run to win. Everyone who competes practices self-discipline in everything. The runners do this to get a crown of leaves that shrivel up and die, but we do it to receive a crown that never dies." (1 Corinthians 9:24-25)

Such wording makes it easy to focus on the finish line, because races always have distinct endings. And once they're over, you get to take a break. So we focus on getting across that finish line with little thought as to what happens next and how that might affect our story now. We think that if we can just get to heaven, we can collapse onto streets of gold, sporting custom-fitted robes and a plug-n-play harp.

Frankly, if all we are going to do *there and then* is lounge around in robes on precious metals while taking harp lessons,

I'm not all that eager to participate. And I fail to see how that could be much of a prize. I'm sure we'll be singing praises as well, but for an introvert like me, being incessantly surrounded by billions of beings endlessly shouting and chanting doesn't sound much like a heavenly experience.

What if, in addition to some robust singing on occasion, we'll be glorifying God in other ways? And what if how we live *here and now* will position us to best glorify him *there and then*? We'd do better to think of this earthly race, not as our final tour de force, but as more of a preliminary warm-up or a qualifying heat, with implications for the highest experience yet to come.

Remember that in the Philippians passage we do receive an eternal reward for living a life of abundant faith. But what is this crown we receive that can never fade? It's not a conversion experience of saving faith. That's already done. It's not a restored relationship with God—that's already been restored. Other passages describe the faithful being rewarded with a "crown of righteousness" that they then offer back to God to more fully glorify him (2 Timothy 4:8 NKJV; see Revelation 4:10). But physical crowns are temporary things, hardly worthy of the eternal God. So what is it that we could "receive" by living a life of abundant faith that could be offered to God as a way of more fully glorifying him?

Here's a crazy thought: what if the greatest prize you receive *is* the story you will tell of God's abundant provision for you as you lived a life of abundant faith in him? Now that would be something worth offering back to him! There certainly would be no mistaking who would get the credit. We would tell it everywhere, for eternity. And every time we told it to yet another of his children, we would more fully reveal the majesty of God. The story would not even end when we arrive; it would be only just beginning.

I'm not saying that there won't be other rewards for a life full of faith in him, but consider just how valuable your story of abundant faith in the *here and now* will be when you reach the *there and then.*

PREPARE YOUR GEAR

Will your story be worth telling where *and* when *it matters most?*

Activity: Imagine you have arrived in heaven and Moses has just asked you to tell your story. What will you talk about? What stories of God's greatness will you tell? What accounts of his sure and certain promises will you offer as evidence of his faithfulness? What will you be able to say God did through your abundant faith?

Now write down a brief account of the story you want to be able to tell. Be as detailed as possible. Post the story where you can see it and refer to it often to be reminded of the ultimate purpose of living your story here and now.

ABUNDANT FAITH NOW, AMAZING STORY THEN

When we choose to live the life of abundant faith *here and now*, we're intentionally writing an immortal story for *there and then*. If you are going to spend all of eternity telling your story of life lived *here and now*, what parts will be worth telling when all that matters is revealing the majesty of God? If you hesitate to answer, you may suffer from a common ailment amongst Christians known as *SDS: Story Deficiency Syndrome.* The only cure is to let faith open your eyes to step out, step up, and live a different story.

Imagine *then and there* interacting with Moses, whose story is memorialized in Hebrews 11, the Faith Hall of Fame. As you sit beside the crystal sea, Moses strolls up and joins you, his face still glowing slightly from his many encounters with the Almighty. He opens the conversation with a hearty, "So, tell me your story." You happily launch into a brief account of your conversion experience. You describe how your faith had been focused on yourself or someone else, but then God did his mightiest work within you.

"That's great!" Moses replies excitedly. "Isn't God's grace amazing?" But then he leans toward you, rubbing his hands together. "That's an awesome beginning. What happened next? Tell me the rest of your story, of how God showed himself strong when you walked out your life journey with authentic faith!"

You pause, a little confused by his eager query, before mumbling, "Um, well…I…I guess…well, you know, life just sort of…happened." You pause awkwardly, toes curling and uncurling in your heavenly sandals.

Moses pulls back a bit before asking incredulously, "That's it?" You gulp and shift awkwardly before answering.

"Well, yes. I mean, of course, there was, you know, church— and stuff like that."

Blink. Blink. "Oh." There's a long pause as crystal waves splash on crystal shores, while Moses stares incredulously for what seems a millennia. Finally, he shoots a glance at his bare wrist, stands, and begins backing away. "Well, look, I've really got to run," he says. "It's been, um…great talking to you."

Granted, Moses' story is a tough one to beat, but only because he focused his faith on God and answered his call. The same option is open to you. Who wants to be stuck with a boring story for all eternity? Why not live a story in the *here and now* that amazes all who hear it *there and then*?

When your faith is rightly focused, you see that the journey to live a story worth telling is an immortal quest to more fully reveal the majesty of God. It is the pursuit of the very purpose for which you were created: an ever-deepening relationship with your Creator that inspires others to follow as your faith thrives on truth. We can be confident that the faith we live out now will indeed echo throughout eternity, because we will be the ones telling everyone about what God did when we lived a life of abundant faith.

I'm looking forward to hearing your story, my friend, perhaps as we sit together someday and chat with Moses. Isn't it time you joined us on this journey to live a story that's truly worth telling where and when it matters most? Because that is God's reality. Regardless of what you see, sense, or feel, your story can become a classic in eternity. And it can start right now—if only you'll choose the path of the FaithWalker.

EXPLORE THE TRAIL AHEAD

- Think about the story of abundant faith you hope to live. If someone were to describe that story in one sentence, what would it be? Write it down and share it with one of your FaithWalker advisors to help hold you accountable.

- As you reflect on your journey through this book, what are the key action steps you need to take to begin shaping your story into one worth telling for all eternity? List them in order of importance in a place you will see often. Mark your calendar to revisit them in one month to check your progress.

AN INVITATION

If you're ready to live an authentic life of abundant faith, I invite you to join the journey. For additional resources to grow your faith and to connect with others in the FaithWalkers community, visit FaithWalkers.com today.

ACKNOWLEDGMENTS

J ust as the journey to live a story worth telling is one of abundant faith, so this book has been an exercise of trust in God and a host of other people. Very special thanks to my talented assistant, Courtney Coiro, herself a gifted writer, without whom this book could not have been completed. Thank you also to Linda Kardamis (Teach4theHeart.com), Christina Quist, Carole Coiro, and Brittany Studmire for feedback, research, and editing help.

Thank you to the entire team at Abingdon Press, to Lil Copan for her never-ending patience and encouragement, and to Holly Halverson, a truly gifted editor.

Thank you to the following friends to whom I turned for advice along this journey of faith: Dick Savidge (SavidgeAdventures.com), P. Andrew Sandlin (ChristianCulture.com), Hugh Hewitt, John and Mandy Snow, Daniel Buell, Mark Spansel, and Joel J. Miller.

To the following friends, undying gratitude for your support of our faith walk: Darrel and Sandy Simons, Leslie and William C. Blankschaen, John and Lonna Belshaw, Tom and Jaqueline Hardman, Gene and Janet Blackstone, Paul and Linda Bolton,

Paul and Debbie Pineda, Doug and Karen Sumerauer, Tim and Joyce Dalrymple, Kenny Jahng, David and Sandi Ortiz, Dan Selle, Tor Constantino, Cindy Booth—for her unceasing prayer, Mike and Jill Saefkow, Kara and Levi Ali, Andre and Sally Bernier, Frank and Lynda Hester, Lenny and Mario Josef, Amanda Sanchez, Glenn and Josie Leinbach, Branden and Deborah Scattone, Bill and Heather DeLaney, Matt and Faith Montonini, Eric and Chandalyn Frandsen, Ron and Kelly Bissetta, Julie and Mark Belich, David and Kelly Kullberg, Eileen Knowles, and all our friends at Leroy Community Chapel and Cornerstone Christian Academy.

Thanks to the many others who offered encouraging words, a listening ear, and helpful connections: Jeff Goins, Brad Lomenick, Jason Haynes, Mark Cole, David Hoyt, Doug Carter, Skip Prichard, Steve Verleye, Jack Alexander, Bruce and Toni Hebel, Jerry Pacholke, Elizabeth Darling-Ruple, Albert and Judy Alquero, Steve Kaloper, Gary Young, Jared Roach, Bill and Lynde Brownlee, John Smith, Jason Locy, Shannon Milholland, Jennifer Heap, Kevin and Christina Quist, Al and Lisa Storey, David and Laura Duryea, Carina and Johnny Su, Steve Smothermon, Bill Smith, and the many others who've shaped our thoughts and dreams on this journey. If I have forgotten any, please attribute it to my finite memory and not to any shortage of gratitude. May you be doubly blessed by the One who never forgets.

Finally, my endless thanks to my beautiful wife for her love and encouragement—you are still, and always will be, the other side of me—and to all my children for their love, support, and generous sharing of their father for so many nights and weekends. I can't wait to hear the stories your faith will tell.

Notes

Chapter 1: You Can Choose Your Story

"Security does not give purpose."
John Maxwell, *The 5 Levels of Leadership* (New York: Center Street, 2011), 74.

"If we don't change, we don't grow. . . . The real fear should be the opposite course."
Gail Sheehy, *Passages* (New York: E. P. Dutton & Co., Inc., 1974), 416.

Many of us embrace the cultural slogan of whatever.
Steven Garber, *Visions of Vocation: Common Grace for the Common Good* (Downers Grove, IL: InterVarsity Press, 2010), 56.

"We are blown upon the world . . . and as little worth the making."
Mark Twain, "Chapters from My Autobiography," *North American Review*, May 3, 1907.

"Shadow calling"
Steven Pressfield, *Turning Pro: Tap Your Inner Power and Create Your Life's Work* (New York: Black Irish Entertainment, 2012), 13.

"When you wish upon a star . . . make a wish and your dreams will come true."
What came to be Disney's theme song was written by Leigh

Harline and Ned Washington for Walt Disney's 1940 adaptation of *Pinocchio*. The song was first performed by Cliff Edwards.

"All the world is made of faith, and trust, and pixie dust."
J. M. Barrie, quoted on GoodReads.com, http://www.goodreads.com/quotes/28233.

"Moving forward requires great risk... feels more perilous."
Brad Lomenick, *The Catalyst Leader: 8 Essentials for Becoming a Change Maker* (Nashville: Thomas Nelson, 2013), 115.

Chapter 2: Faith Finds a Focus

"He landed safely... all on board survived."
"Flight 1549: A Routine Takeoff Turns Ugly," *CBS News*, February 8, 2009, http://www.cbsnews.com/news/flight-1549-a-routine-takeoff-turns-ugly/.

"N.Y. Jet Crash Called 'Miracle on the Hudson,'" *NBC News*, January 15, 2009, http://www.nbcnews.com/id/28678669/ns/us_news-life/t/ny-jet-crash-called-miracle-hudson/.

"If God did not exist, it would be necessary to invent him."
Voltaire, "Épître à l'Auteur du Livre des Trois Imposteurs" or "Letter to the Author of The Three Impostors," 1770, translated by Jack Iverson at http://www.whitman.edu/VSA/trois.imposteurs.html. "The physical world... we know it's false."

"The physical world provides no room... we know it's false."
Marvin Minsky, *The Society of Mind* (New York: Simon & Schuster, 1985), 307.

"If you just believe."
Josh Groban, "Believe," *The Polar Express: Original Motion Picture Soundtrack* (Warner Sunset Records, 2004). Lyrics written by Glen Ballard and Alan Silvestri.

"The thing about trains... deciding to get on."
Robert Zemeckis, *The Polar Express* (Warner Brothers, 2004).

Chapter 3: Faith Makes Your Story Worth Telling

"He's dead.... Look for loose change."
The Princess Bride, special edition (Santa Monica, CA: MGM

Home Entertainment, 2001). Original film released in 1987, screenplay by William Goldman.

"Monotony is the awful reward of the careful."
A. G. Buckham, quoted in Eric Wagner, "57 Timeless Quotes for 2013," *Forbes*, December 18, 2012, http://www.forbes.com/sites/ericwagner/2012/12/18/57-timeless-quotes-for-2013/.

"Great faith enables…little faith in a little god."
E. M. Bounds, *The Complete Works of E. M. Bounds on Prayer* (Grand Rapids: Baker Books, 2004), 175.

"God is glorified in…a dependence of the redeemed on him."
Jonathan Edwards, "God Glorified in Man's Dependence," sermon in Boston, MA, on July 8, 1731, http://www.monergism.com/thethreshold/sdg/edwards/edwards_mandependence.html. Text also found in *The Works of Jonathan Edwards*, volume 2 (Carlisle, PA: The Banner of Truth Trust, 1997), 3.

"This is how God works…display his greatness."
David Platt, *Radical* (Colorado Springs, CO: Multnomah Publishers, 2010), 48.

Chapter 4: Faith Opens Your Eyes

"Great! Where are we going?"
The Lord of the Rings: The Fellowship of the Ring (New Line Cinema/Warner Brothers, 2001). Screenplay by Fran Walsh, Philippa Boyens, and Peter Jackson.

Thomas became the first missionary…a true FaithWalker.
"The Acts of Thomas" from *The Apocryphal New Testament*, trans. M. R. James (Oxford: Clarendon Press, 1924), http://www.earlychristianwritings.com/text/actsthomas.html.

Goliath likely suffered…hand-to-hand combat.
Malcolm Gladwell, *David and Goliath* (New York: Little, Brown and Company, 2013).

"If you're bored,…the footsteps of Christ."
Mark Batterson, *In a Pit with a Lion on a Snowy Day* (Sisters, OR: Multnomah Publishers, 2006), 57.

"The most magical place on Earth."
    Disney's tagline at http://www.visitdisney.com/history.html.

"It's kind of fun to do the impossible."
    Walt Disney quoted in Derek Walker, *Animated Architecture,*
    architectural design profile (New York: St. Martin's Press,
    1982), 10.

Chapter 5: Faith Thrives on Truth

*To be Lieutenant General Yoshitsugu Saito....first of many sui-
cides that day.*
    "Battle of Saipan," *History Channel,* http://www.history.com
    /topics/world-war-ii/battle-of-saipan.

To convince Japanese soldiers...and pulled the pin.
    "Biography: Koyu Shiroma," *Victory in the Pacific,* PBS, 2013,
    http://www.pbs.org/wgbh/americanexperience/features/biogra
    phy/pacific-koyu-shiroma/.

    Bill Hoover, "Saipan, the Last Days of the Battle," Veterans
    History Project, http://www.kilroywashere.org/003-Pages
    /Hoover/03-Hoover-TheLast.html.

The logos from which we derive our word logic.
    Thayer and Smith, Greek lexicon entry for "Logos," *The KJV
    New Testament Greek Lexicon,* http://www.biblestudytools
    .com/lexicons/greek/kjv/logos.html.

"A light to you in dark places, when all other lights go out."
    J. R. R. Tolkien, *The Fellowship of the Ring* (New York: Del
    Rey, 2012), 423.

Two of the best resources...
    Gordon D. Fee and Douglas Stuart, *How to Read the Bible for
    All It's Worth,* 4th ed., (Grand Rapids: Zondervan, 2014).

    R. C. Sproul, *Knowing Scripture,* rev. ed. (Downers Grove, IL:
    InterVarsity Press, 2009).

A good tool to guide...any translation.
    *The Chronological Guide to the Bible: Explore God's Word in
    Historical Order* (Nashville: Thomas Nelson, 2010).

More than seven hundred people…Bible every day.
Ben Irwin, "Biblica Launches Institute for Bible Reading to Address Growing Crisis of Bible Engagement," PRWeb.com (Colorado Springs, CO), January 24, 2014, http://www.prweb .com/releases/2014/01/prweb11518591.htm.

With the many…truth in Scripture.
Here are some tools to help you dig deeper into your study of the Bible. BibleGateway.com has a topical index, devotionals, reading plans, commentaries, dictionaries, audio and video resources—and it's also available as a mobile app. Crosswalk .com/faith/bible-study features articles and blogs, daily devotionals, Bible study notes, and a growing community. www .BibleStudyTools.com has concordances, Bible search, lexicons, and videos. Lumina.bible.org has an interactive layout for reading and study side-by-side. Read reviews for more sites at http:// www.christianwebsite.com/top-5-online-bible-study-tools/.

Chapter 6: Faith Finds a Voice

I decided that…for a dozen years.
For more information about Cornerstone Christian Academy, visit http://www.cca-impact.info.

"Sometimes what we perceive…a providential pause."
Mark Batterson, *The Circle Maker: Praying Circles Around Your Biggest Dreams and Greatest Fears* (Grand Rapids: Zondervan, 2011), 89.

"Far in the sameness of the woods."
Robert Frost, "The Demiurge's Laugh," *A Boy's Will* (New York: Henry Holt & Co., 1915), 54.

"Struggle opens up…rescue and redemption."
Chuck DeGroat, *Leaving Egypt: Finding God in the Wilderness Places* (Grand Rapids: Square Inch, 2011), 159.

"Prayer is faith passing into action."
Richard Cecil, quoted in *Reflections on the Lord's Prayer*, ed. Susan Brower (Grand Rapids: Zondervan, 2009), 93.

"Faith is to the soul…is past my comprehension too."

J.C. Ryle, "A Call To Prayer," sermon, http://www.gracegems
.org/SERMONS/call_to_prayer.htm.

"Prayer and faith...always believing."
E. M. Bounds, *The Complete Works of E. M. Bounds on Prayer*
(Grand Rapids: Baker Books, 2004), 166.

"The greatest tragedy...they go unasked."
Batterson, *The Circle Maker*, 17.

"We tend to use prayer...in sync with ours."
Oswald Chambers, *Prayer: A Holy Occupation*, Kindle ed.
(Discovery House, 2010), introduction.

"Prayer is...him who prays."
Bounds, *Complete Works*, 213.

"You can do more than pray...have prayed."
Dr. A. J. Gordon, quoted in E. M. Bounds, *E. M. Bounds on
Prayer* (Peabody, MA: Hendrickson Publishers, 2006), 179.

The word translated "pour" literally means "to empty it all out."
Brown, Driver, Briggs, and Gesenius, Hebrew lexicon entry for
"Shaphak," *The KJV Old Testament Hebrew Lexicon*, http://
www.biblestudytools.com/lexicons/hebrew/kjv/shaphak.html.

"In prayer...words without a heart."
John Bunyan, quoted in Warren Wiersbe, *The Wiersbe Bible
Commentary: Old Testament* (Colorado Springs, CO: David C.
Cook, 2007), 1018. Also quoted in Martin H. Manser, ed., *The
Westminster Collection of Christian Quotations* (Louisville,
KY: Westminster John Knox Press, 2001), 288.

"It is more important...change my circumstances."
Tim Elmore and John Hull, *Pivotal Praying* (Nashville: Nelson
Books, 2002), 87.

"He who kneels the most, stands the best."
"D. L. Moody Quotes," SermonIndex.net, http://www.sermon
index.net/modules/articles/index.php?view=article&aid=33025.

"Whenever you face...is deteriorating."
Bryan Lowe, "T. D. Jakes—Some of the Best Quotes,"

CrossQuotes.org, January 22, 2014, http://crossquotes.org
/category/t-d-jakes/.

"God doesn't call us...doesn't come through."
Francis Chan, *Crazy Love*, 2nd ed. (Colorado Springs, CO:
David C. Cook, 2013), 122.

"The greatest enemy of hunger for God is not poison but apple pie."
John Piper, *A Hunger for God* (Wheaton, IL: Crossway, 1997),
14.

Much research...she were drunk.
Phil LeBeau, "Texting And Driving Worse Than Drinking and
Driving," CNBC (2009), http://www.cnbc.com/id/31545004.
David L. Strayer, Frank A. Drews, and Dennis J. Crouch, "A
Comparison of the Cell Phone Driver and the Drunk Driver,"
Human Factors, 48, no. 2 (Summer 2006), 381–91.

"I have so much...in prayer."
Martin Luther, quoted in Bounds, *E. M. Bounds on Prayer*,
179–80.

"The shortening...too late hours."
Robert Isaac Wilberforce and Samuel Wilberforce, *The Life of
William Wilberforce by His Sons*, vol. 4 (London: John Murray
[John Childs], 1838), 162. Google Books. For more on Wilber-
force and his impact, see Eric Metaxas's excellent biography
*Amazing Grace: William Wilberforce and the Heroic Campaign
to End Slavery* (New York: HarperCollins, 2007).

Chapter 7: Faith Answers the Call

Christina and Kevin Quist's story
Jeremy Statton, "The Quist Family: A Secretly Incredible, 'Normal' Family," on LivingBetterStories.com, August 2012, http://
www.jeremystatton.com/quist-family. Italics added.

"True faith rests...said it."
A. W. Tozer, *Man: The Dwelling Place of God* (Fig Books,
2013), 23. Also A. W. Tozer, *Man: The Dwelling Place of God*,
Biblesnet.com, http://www.biblesnet.com/AW%20Tozer%20

Man%20-%20The%20Dwelling%20Place%20of%20God.pdf, 16.

Some years ago . . . the church today.
Associated Press, "Mayor Campbell Announces Cleveland Adopt-a-Can Plan," 19ActionNews.com, 2004, http://www .19actionnews.com/story/1597657/mayor-campbell-announces -cleveland-adopt-a-can-plan.

"Not all of us . . . with great love."
Mother Teresa, quoted in Brian Kolodiejchuk, ed., *Mother Teresa: Come Be My Light* (New York: Doubleday Religion, 2007), 34.

"We are all failures—at least the best of us are."
J. M. Barrie, rectorial address at St. Andrew's University, Scotland, May 3, 1922. *Columbia World of Quotations* (Columbia University Press, 1996), Dictionary.com, http://quotes.dictio nary.com/We_are_all_failures_at_least_all_the.

"Good is the enemy of great."
Jim Collins, *Good to Great* (New York: HarperBusiness, 2001), 1.

"You must give up to go up."
John Maxwell, *The 21 Irrefutable Laws of Leadership*, rev. and updated ed. (Nashville: Thomas Nelson, 2007), 219.

"Faith does not . . . where man's power ends."
George Müeller, quoted in Ron Rhodes, *1001 Unforgettable Quotes About God, Faith, and the Bible* (Eugene, OR: Harvest House Publishers, 2011), 83.

Chapter 8: Faith Moves You to Move Mountains

"Men and women are . . . prove Him now."
E. M. Bounds, *The Classic Collection on Prayer* (Orlando, FL: Bridge-Logos, 2001), 428.

The Hebrew word translated . . . knowing by observing.
Brown, Driver, Briggs and Gesenius, Hebrew lexicon entry for "Yada`," *The KJV Old Testament Hebrew Lexicon*, http://www .biblestudytools.com/lexicons/hebrew/kjv/yada.html.

Chapter 9: Faith Keeps Moving Forward

Glenn Cunningham didn't even...who never quit.
Summarized from Glenn Cunningham, *Never Quit* (Grand Rapids: Chosen Books, 1981).

Chapter 10: Faith Changes Everything

"Reality is God's home address."
Frederica Matthews-Green, "Escape from Fantasy Island," *Christianity Today*, July 12, 1999, http://www.christianitytoday .com/ct/1999/july12/9t8058.html.

To contribute a verse to the "powerful play."
Walt Whitman, "O Me! O Life!" *Leaves of Grass*, ed. Jerome Loving, World's Classics 1892 edition (Oxford: Oxford University Press, 1990), 215.

"The legacy of heroes...a great example."
Benjamin Disraeli Letters: 1848–1851 (Toronto: University of Toronto Press Inc, 1993), 149.

"You have never...everlasting splendors."
C. S. Lewis, *The Weight of Glory* (New York: HarperOne, 2009), 46.

"Here's a crazy thought: what if the greatest prize you receive is the story...."
Special thanks for inspiration to David Kullberg, *Winning the War: God's Plan for Victory and the Defeat of Evil in this Present Age*, 2014.